A CELEBRATION OF EMPIRE

 Spellmount Publishers
in association with the
Victorian Military Society

A Centenary Celebration of
the Diamond Jubilee of Queen Victoria
1837 - 1897

by Colonel Peter Walton

Contents

British Library Cataloguing in
Publication Data
A catalogue record for this book is
available from the British Library

Copyright © Peter Walton 1997

ISBN 1-86227-021-X

First published in the UK in 1997 by:
Spellmount Limited
The Old Rectory
Staplehurst
Kent TN12 0AZ

Design by Ian Hughes

Printed in the United Kingdom
by Ecran Offset Limited

List of Illustrations

Preface

At 2 am on 20th June 1837, King William IV expired and thus propelled his niece to the Throne. Princess Alexandrina Victoria of Kent became Queen Victoria of Great Britain and Ireland and, from 1st January 1877, Empress of India. She ruled for sixty three years and seven months, dying at the age of 81 on 22nd January 1901.

If those few simple words can be said to summarise the reign of Queen Victoria they certainly obscure a story which is remarkable in every dimension. This book was conceived as a celebration by the Victorian Military Society of the Diamond Jubilee which occurred in June 1897. But interesting as an account of the grand events of a century ago would be, there was a need to place them in a context. Newspapers tell us that our children pass through school without encountering Nelson, Wellington, Roberts or Kitchener: what, one wonders, do they know of the industrial revolutions of the Victorian age, of India and the Empire? How can one understand what is happening in the world today or hope to perceive the attitudes and possible intentions of those who influence great events without having a plain knowledge of the past? What are we all to make of 1997 as the United Kingdom Year of the Commonwealth, as the year we ceded Hong Kong back to the Chinese people and surrendered our lease to the New Territories, as the 50th Anniversary of the Independence of India and Pakistan, if we do not know how these first came about? The Victorian Military Society stands for education, and naturally for the harmless and pleasurable pursuits of its members. It does not stand for political observation and it has no view at all on the rightness or otherwise of Empire: these are matters for individuals whose freedom to express them (though not any license to thrust them) is still a priceless boon of life in this country. The Society welcomes the establishment of The Empire and Commonwealth Museum in Brunel's Station building in Bristol and warmly supports its curatorial and educational aims and objectives.

The material in this book has been drawn from many sources, Appendix 1 very largely from the London Gazette, and the illustrations from the contemporary press and from private collections. While in some cases better photographs are to be found in public museum collections, their reproduction charges are now so high as to be prohibitive for a publication of this kind. On the other hand, the capabilities of the newest computers to "restore" picture quality, for example from newsprint dot-matrix back to something close to the original, are now quite stunning as the reader will find. The colour picture in the centre is after a drawing by Frank Dadd and originally appeared as a 3ft by 2ft Supplement to The Graphic. The bibliography at the end of the book may be of help to the reader who would like to know more. Of course, for those who find any of the military information a lure, membership of the Victorian Military Society can be recommended; a note about this is elsewhere.

The author is very grateful indeed to a number of people who have helped to make this book possible: Chris Kempton has unearthed mysteries of the Indian Army and Bryan Maggs has kindly loaned photographs from his collection; Mark Reid of the Canadian War Museum in Ottawa has been voluminously helpful with information from his sources; David Horn of the Guards Museum has provided contemporary press material; The Daily Mail has kindly given permission for the reproduction of the article by G W Steevens; Ian Hughes has designed and set the book, and put up with the author's unreasonable expectations; and Jamie Wilson of Spellmount has been generous in the support which has made publication a possibility despite a lead time of weeks rather than months, or years!

Tenterden, Kent   Peter Walton
June 1997

Queen Victoria

Princess Alexandrine Victoria was born at Kensington Palace in London on 24th May 1819. She was the only child of His Royal Highness the Duke of Kent and Strathearne. Her grandfather was King George III who was then in the fifty-ninth year of his reign as King of Great Britain and Ireland and also King of Hanover. In fact he was King only in name having suffered for many years from a form of dementia. The constitutional reins of government were as a result in the hands of the Princess's uncle George, Prince of Wales and Prince Regent. The new Princess was not immediately in the line of succession for she had two uncles and their descendants before her. But of these, the Prince Regent had lost his only daughter, the Princess Charlotte, in November 1817 while William, Duke of Clarence, had lost one daughter in infancy and was shortly to lose another. When King George III died on 29th January 1820, the Prince Regent became King George IV. He reigned for ten years to be succeeded by his brother of Clarence, as King William IV. By then Princess Victoria was, so long as she survived, next in line to the Throne. She was just 18 years old when her uncle died on 20th June 1837.

Very soon after her birth, the Princess Victoria was deprived of her father, the Duke of Kent who died on 23rd January 1820. An only child, she was brought up by her mother who was the daughter of the Duke of Saxe-Coburg-Gotha and the widow of the Prince of Leiningen. The Duke of Kent, when he died, left only debts and the Princess's mother was not rich. The household was therefore run on modest lines. More testingly, though, the young Princess Victoria was kept in seclusion from visiting children and grown-ups alike, ignorant even of her royal destiny. Her mother, who may have hoped to have been Regent for at least a while, kept very strict control. She even refused the Princess a bedroom of her own. Princess Victoria's uncle, Prince Leopold, afterwards the first King of Belgium, took the place of her father and her education was entrusted to the Baroness Lehzen and Dr Davys, afterwards Bishop of Peterborough. It is recorded that by the age of twelve, she was getting on well with Latin, French and German and had begun Greek and Italian.

She had not, however, been introduced to History or Current Affairs so that it was with some surprise that she discovered from a genealogical table in a book that she was the King's heir. Although she later described her childhood as "sad", the impenetrably protective treatment she received did not inhibit her willingness to learn nor her interest

in and concern for others. In May 1837, her coming of age was celebrated at Court with a Ball at St James's Palace. King William was too unwell to attend but wrote offering her an allowance of £10,000 a year as his heir. But in fact he was more ill than was thought and on June 14th there was a serious turn for the worse. By the 18th, Waterloo Day, he was sinking fast though he found the strength to receive from the Duke of Wellington the banner which the latter presents annually to the Sovereign in return for his estates. At 2 am on the 20th June, the King died. The British crown passed to his niece while that of Hanover which could not pass to a female was inherited by his brother Cumberland.

The story of how the Princess was woken at 5 am to receive the Lord Chamberlain and the Archbishop of Canterbury is probably well known. But it loses nothing in the telling for the new Queen if young and dishevelled at such an hour was pretty and composed, two qualities which all can admire. A little later, suitably briefed by the Prime Minister, she was ready to face her first Privy Council. Tiny but dignified and dressed in black, she took the oath, received the homage of her two surviving royal uncles and of other dignitaries, and read a speech.

The scene was recorded not only by the artist Sir David Wilkie (who got into trouble for painting the Queen in a white dress in order to emphasise her innocence) but also by many of those who were there: the unanimous impression was of her grace, modesty, charm and self-possession. Not yet suspected, perhaps, were other attributes including strength of character (though she remained shy throughout her life), attention to detail, and a formidable memory. The Queen greatly depended on her first Prime Minister Lord Melbourne but despite her lack of years and of experience of the world she was not slow to make up her mind nor to express her opinions. An early decision was to remove her bed from her mother's room and to send away her mother's Secretary, the pompous Sir John Conroy. She suspected that her mother was his mistress and she hated him; her mother never regained influence over her.

The day after the Accession, the Queen went with her mother to St James's Palace where at 10 am the Proclamation was read. After the ceremony, Lord Melbourne presented the new Queen to the people from a window overlooking the central courtyard. There were loud cheers and the Queen, dressed in black

Figure 3. Queen Victoria at eighteen and the Prince Consort at about the same age.

mourning, curtsied her thanks while tears of emotion ran down her cheeks. In the light of subsequent events it is interesting to note that among the crowd that day was Daniel O'Connell, the Irish patriot, who made himself hoarse cheering the "beloved young lady by whom England's throne is now filled". Most of the nation had yet of course to hear of these events let alone to see the Queen but it seems probable that their sentiments would have been much the same. This certainly went for the Navy and Army. The troops on duty for the Proclamation would have been the first to see their new young Sovereign and on that day would have been established the first glimmering of that mutual love and respect which were to bind the Services to her throughout her long reign.

Around this time, it was recorded that the Queen "gets up soon after eight o'clock, breakfasts in her own room and employs the whole morning in transacting business. She reads all the despatches and has every matter of interest and importance in every department laid before her. At eleven or twelve Melbourne comes to her and stays an hour, more or less, according to the business he may have to transact. At two she rides with a large suite (and she likes to have it numerous); Melbourne always rides at her left hand and the Equerry in Waiting generally on the right. She rides for two hours along the road and the greater part of the time at a full gallop. After riding she amuses herself for the rest of the afternoon with music and singing, playing and romping with children ... or in any other way she fancies. The hour for dinner is nominally half past seven o'clock..." Later accounts, with the benefit of the objective eye of distance, note that she often stayed in bed for half the morning probably because she had been up dancing with her suite until the small hours. The riding was a passion and an elegant figure the Queen made riding side-saddle with a long flowing habit and a feather in her hat. For military occasions, she had a little scarlet jacket.

The Queen developed a liking for ceremony which lasted throughout her reign. Probably because she was shy, her Court was more formal than that of King William before her. But during the late summer of 1837 she gained much pleasure from local expeditions bowling through the countryside in her carriage with a cavalry escort. Everywhere she was received with

enthusiasm, nowhere more so than in the City of London to which she made her first State Visit on 9th November. She travelled in a coach with eight cream-coloured horses and was met at Temple Bar (then in Fleet Street but since removed to stand forlornly

in a field in Oxfordshire) by the Lord Mayor who presented the keys of the City. On 20th November, the Queen opened her first Parliament in person: more troops and ceremonial, but also an opportunity to see the people and to be seen. All this was a foretaste for her Coronation which took place in Westminster Abbey on 28th June 1838.

The day dawned dull and rainy. But a crowd of some 400,000 people filled the streets and nothing was going to damp their enthusiasm. As the procession began from Buckingham Palace just before 10 am, the sun broke through. "Queen's weather" as this English phenomenon became known never failed her throughout her reign; the sun always appeared for great occasions. The Coronation procession passed along Piccadilly, St James's Street, Pall Mall and Whitehall to Westminster Abbey. The crowds demonstrated their pleasure

and loyalty, attracted as much perhaps to the Duke of Wellington, a well known figure, as to the new young Queen. At the Abbey door, she was received by the Bishop of Bath and Wells and the Bishop of Durham who conducted her to the throne facing the Altar. Unfortunately, all did not go precisely according to plan: during the homage, the Queen was moved to step down from the throne to help the aged Lord Rolle who stumbled and rolled over as he knelt down; the Archbishop of Canterbury thrust the ruby ring on to the wrong finger, which hurt! But perhaps worse, he managed to set the crown on her head back to front. Nonetheless, the Queen very much enjoyed the whole day and wrote a very long and entertaining account of it in her journal. It was after 6 pm by the time the Queen returned to the Palace, 8 by the time dinner was served and well past 11 by the time she retired, though not to bed: instead she watched the fireworks in Green Park until after midnight. Lord Melbourne, her guide, mentor and very much her senior, was exhausted.

It was of great constitutional importance that the Queen should marry. The suggestion that her consort should be her cousin, Prince Albert of Saxe-Coburg, had already been considered. In 1836, he had come to England with his brother. In 1839 he came again and this time the Queen fell in love with him. Born on 26th August 1819, he was in fact some months younger than the Queen. But in demeanour he was considerably older; he was well educated, travelled, methodical, hard working and to the English who came to admire his worth, just a bit boring. But to the Queen, he was – aside from her duty – everything, and she took him to her heart with gusto:

Figure 4. The Marriage of the Queen to Prince Albert, 10th February 1840.

"Albert's beauty is most striking", she exclaimed. With an eye to her relative seniority, it was she who proposed though it has to be said with some embarrassment. But of course she was accepted and the marriage was fixed for 10th February the next year. Arriving at Dover on his way from Coburg for the ceremony, the Prince was met by an escort of the 11th Light Dragoons who were in due course rewarded with the title 11th (Prince Albert's Own) Hussars. The day of the wedding dawned wet but magically cleared later as the Queen and her Prince emerged from the Chapel Royal St James's Palace after the ceremony. Then it was off by carriage to Windsor. Four days later, to the bridegroom's disappointment, the Queen decided that the honeymoon was over and they returned to Buckingham Palace.

The marriage lasted for 21 years until Prince Albert died, worn out, of typhoid fever in 1861. This period was remarkable in many ways. An early preoccupation was with the production of a family: the Princess Royal arrived in November 1840 and by 1846 there were five children. After the first, the Queen had complained: "men never think, at least seldom think, what a hard task it is for us women to go through with this very often". She then proceeded to have eight more children. Meanwhile, Albert was wrestling with the problems of joining a Court at which he had no formal position and a country which was not too sure that it wanted him. Two days before the marriage, it was announced that he had been appointed a Field Marshal: the United Service Journal was outraged. "The generous Prince", it shouted "himself blazing with decorations and at the summit of military rank, though he has not yet won his spurs nor served in a single grade, will learn with surprise, and doubtless repeat to the Sovereign that the remnant of those who in subordinate grades fought and bled for her throne and family – for their land and liberty, continue undistinguished by any mark of service save their scars,

unnoted by the smallest token of their country's gratitude." Whether it was fair, so early in his stay in his adopted country, to take him to task in this way is a good question. If it was presentationally unfortunate that the only significant honour conferred on the occasion of the Queen's marriage was to her husband and he a foreigner, it was certainly an opportunity for the Press to air a grievance. This was real: the only reward for officers after long service, wounds and ill-health, was half-pay, provided they qualified; for non-commissioned ranks who had

Figure 5. The Queen riding in military costume at Aldershot.

not served long enough to qualify for a tiny pension, there was nothing. Except for those who had fought at Waterloo a quarter of a century before, there was not even a medal. It was indeed a stain on the nation's honour that soldiers and sailors should be simply thrown on the mercy of the community when discharged. That many were forced to beg or to turn to crime was hardly surprising though such is the perversity of human nature that their condition often brought them abuse rather than relief. But it is worth noting that although better support for discharged servicemen remained far in the future, only another seven years were to elapse before something was done about recognition. A Military General Service Medal was authorised in 1847 mainly for the battles of the Napoleonic Wars (1793-1814) and a Naval equivalent for the same Wars but including actions up to the Bombardment of Acre in 1840, one of the very few Naval actions of the Victorian period and the last involving sailing ships. Even more imaginative was the institution of the Victoria Cross in 1856. The idea of a supreme award for individual gallantry in the face of the enemy, regardless of rank, originated with the Prince Consort and was willingly adopted by the Queen. The public occasions at which she presented the first VCs and a number of Crimean War medals were of great significance in bonding the forces to the Queen.

Within the Household, Prince Albert was obliged to begin with a staff selected for him by the Queen. He was not allowed to make any decisions, a hard trial for any husband, let alone an intelligent man of his capabilities. But gradually he brought the Queen to his way of thinking and after some while was able to embark on reforms, at first of Palace management, and then wider afield. The English continued to object to his German ways especially his inability to relax in company but in the end they were obliged to admire his many skills and accomplishments. Among them he was a musician and a connoisseur of music who brought concerts to the Court and gave wider encouragement; he was a patron of the arts who furthered the work of architects, sculptors, painters and others, and added importantly to the Royal Collection; he appreciated his position as Chancellor of Cambridge University and took an active interest in academic affairs; he himself designed houses for the poor and exhibited in many ways an enlightened view of the social problems of his day; he not only reformed

Figure 6. Distribution of Crimea Medals by the Queen at Horse Guards, 26th May 1855.

the archaic administration of the Royal Palaces but turned his energies to the efficient management of the Royal Estates as well. Probably the jewel in his crown was the Great Exhibition of 1851, the first truly International Exhibition ever arranged, coupled with its sequel, the creation of the South Kensington complex of museums and colleges: what has been called Albertopolis. Nor did he neglect the Armed Forces. Despite his inauspicious start in 1840, he had in fact great influence for good particularly with the Army. Not all his ideas were crowned with success, such as his design for a new cap of conical form with a turned down brim to protect the soldier from sun and rain alike: universally unpopular, this became the butt of Punch cartoons such as the series devoted to "The Brook Green Volunteer". But men went to war in the Crimea

in other confections, his infantry shako, the "Albert pot", and his cavalry "Albert helmet". A more important area of concern was field training and manoeuvres, and it had something to do with Prince Albert's influence that the first "camp of exercise" was established at Chobham in the summer of 1853. From this successful experiment grew the development of nearby Aldershot from an initial purchase in 1853 of 3000 acres to the present military town with its outlying facilities and its vital contribution to military preparedness over almost 150 years. His position was bolstered by honours: he was appointed Colonel of the Scots Fusilier Guards in 1842, Captain General of the Honourable Artillery Company in 1843 and in 1850 Colonel in Chief of the 60th Rifles; in September 1852 he succeeded the Duke of Wellington as Colonel of the Grenadier Guards and as Colonel in Chief of the Rifle Brigade, surrendering his Colonelcy in Chief of the 60th at the same time. More practically, his hand was also in the Volunteer movement of 1859-60 to face what was thought at the time to be a threat of French invasion. Although the crisis soon passed the enthusiasm of the population did not; corps of Rifle Volunteers sprang up all over the country, totalling by May 1860 some 124,000 men or rather more again than the strength of the regular Army of the day. Although the fortunes of this popular movement waxed and waned over the next 50 years, it became in the end a crucially important component of the Territorial Force formed in 1908. It was this Volunteer strength which supplemented the Regular Army in the first grim year of the Great War of 1914-19, giving vital time for the formation of the vast citizen armies which gained the eventual victory.

The Crimean War when Britain, France and Sardinia sided with Turkey against Russia began in confusion and high hopes in 1854. Confusion led predictably to administrative and tactical disasters but there was also some success and eventually a political settlement which met at least partially the war aims of the Allies. The Queen was much afflicted by the suffering of her troops and both she and the Prince Consort paid great attention to the medical arrangements. She commissioned photographs of the wounded and visited them, going twice in the space of a few days in March 1855 to the hospital in Chatham. No sooner was the Crimea over than the Indian Mutiny broke out in 1857, succeeded by the 1860 campaign in China. The Queen's anguish for her soldiers was much reported and she gave what support she could.

But in December 1861, Prince Albert died of typhoid fever for which, it was said, the appalling drains at Windsor were responsible. In truth, though only 42, the Prince Consort was worn out and for two years had been struggling with sheer exhaustion. The effect of this tragedy on the Queen was dramatic. She retreated into mourning and privacy, almost abandoning public engagements altogether. She gave out that life could not be expected to go on as before: family events were overshadowed by the absence of her husband and public ones became anathema. But despite herself she was charmed by Princess Alexandra to whom the Prince of Wales was married at Windsor in March 1863. Then, exactly 10 years after the death of her husband, her son fell ill of typhoid too and for a while his life was in the balance. Fortunately he recovered and both the Prince and Princess of Wales accompanied her to a formal Thanksgiving Service at St Paul's in February 1872. But this was a rare outing and the people led by the Press grumbled at her unreasonable seclusion. But as with any abnormal behaviour, perceptions of it grew out of proportion. It is of course true that she maintained her attitude of grief-stricken mourning far beyond any reasonable period; it is true too that she was shy; and it is true that she was difficult to her Ministers and her staff, except perhaps for her favourites (which made it worse!). But she was not unmindful of her role and duty as Sovereign and while she often obstructed and irritated those around her, she did play her part at Windsor especially. She was neither idle nor unconcerned and her sense of humour remained in excellent order for as long as she lived. If the public did not see her, visiting monarchs, diplomats and others did. One such visit was by the Shah of Persia (now called Iran) who, it was said, had never been told that he should not "put his fingers into dishes, or take food out of his mouth again to look at it after it has been chewed, or fling it under the table if it does not suit his taste" nor indeed that he should not make attempts to console himself for the absence of his harem. Not surprisingly the Queen was reluctant to agree a date for his visit. But to her credit she did and it went off extremely well: the Shah ate mostly fruit which reduced the possibilities for embarrassment, he wore the most extravagant dress with ruby buttons on his diamond encrusted coat, and he responded to investment with the Garter by presenting two Orders in return. But because such visits were largely unseen, it was a matter of

Figure 7. The arrival of the Shah of Persia at Windsor, 20th June 1873.

profound relief to the public that she felt able to appear at the celebrations of her Golden Jubilee in 1887. Not only the long reigning Queen and Empress of her own dominions but also "grandmother of Europe" by virtue of the interlinking marriages of her large family, the Queen could command the attention of the world. From all parts came gifts and addresses to the Queen and London became the headquarters of Kings and Heirs-Apparent of almost every European State during the festivities. The climax was the special Thanksgiving Service in Westminster Abbey on 21st June. She was conveyed to it and returned to Buckingham Palace in a magnificent procession featuring troops from all parts of her Empire and, a special gesture, a bodyguard of 18 Princes and Royal Dukes of whom 3 were her sons, six were sons-in-law and nine were grandsons or grandsons-in-law. The most conspicuous figure, it was reported, was Crown Prince Frederick of Prussia, husband of the Queen's eldest daughter and father of the future Kaiser William II. The crowds were ecstatic, the sun shone, and the Queen seemed once more to be alive. A banner proclaiming "Good Sovereign – no change required" seemed to sum up the public's attitude and to bid farewell to a mournful and withdrawn quarter century.

Although protocol and formality were not relaxed at Court, the Queen's sense of humour occasionally shone through. One of the trials for her Household was that when the Queen finished eating a course, everyone's plates were removed whether or not they had finished. One evening the Queen had Lord Hartington beside her and while they were getting on well he was doing more of the talking and less of the eating. Inevitably she finished first with the result that his food was whisked away. In the middle of a sentence he shot over his shoulder: "Here, bring that back!" Stunned, the Household held its breath but the Queen only smiled. On another occasion, an ancient Admiral was telling the Queen about his time in the Navy when she interposed a question about the Admiral's sister whom she knew. Unfortunately, the old sailor was a little deaf and while he got the thrust of the question he had not realised that the subject had been changed. Thinking that the Queen was still interested in his ship, he held that if he had his way he would turn her over and scrape her bottom! The Household prepared to hold its breath only to see the Queen convulsed with laughter until her eyes streamed. Yet another example shows that her human emotions were not too far below the surface: she was fond of relating how one starlit night at Windsor she had opened her bedroom window to look out and a sentry at the foot of the Castle wall, thinking she was a housemaid, began to address her in "most affectionate and endearing" terms. The Queen at once drew her curtains but was quite delighted at what had happened.

During the last fourteen years of her life, she made a number of visits to the Continent including Berlin to call on her daughter and son-in-law, and to Biarritz, Aix-les-Bains, Grasses, Florence, Coburg, Darmstadt and, increasingly regularly, the South of France. She was at Nice in the Spring of 1897 which was to be the busiest of the closing years of her reign. On her way home, she granted an audience to the

President of France at a suburban railway station near Paris (which is something of a comment in itself on the way in which she and her international position were viewed at this time). On 10th May she made a highly successful visit to London and on the 21st another to Sheffield. In June and July she was occupied with the many events of the Diamond Jubilee celebrations after which she went to Osborne House. She received there the King of Siam. Later she spent the autumn as was customary at Balmoral. Early in 1898, solicitous as ever for her troops, she paid several visits to the Royal Victoria Hospital at Netley on Southampton Water during one of which she presented the Victoria Cross to Piper Findlater of the Gordon Highlanders and Private Vickery of the Dorsets. Both were heroes of the campaign to quell the Great Rising on the North West Frontier of 1897-98; there were also wounded from Benin in West Africa and from the Sudan. It had been a busy year for the Army. In March the Queen went off to the South of France for her Spring holiday and in the autumn to Balmoral as usual; the intervening months were quiet. In the Spring of 1899 she went again as normal to the South of France. On 17th May, back in London, she laid the Foundation Stone for the Victoria and Albert Museum, a development which gave her special pleasure. On the 6th July she presented New Colours to 3rd Battalion Coldstream Guards at the beginning of a visit to the Army in Aldershot. On the 15th, back at Windsor, she presented a State Colour to the Scots Guards. Later in the year she reviewed the Foot Guards on the eve of their departure to the Anglo-Boer War in South Africa. On the 1st January 1900, she noted in her journal her fears for her family and her forces and her hopes that she might yet live a while with all her faculties and "to a certain extent" her eyesight! In March she cheered her subjects by coming to London and driving through the City and the West End where she was received with tumultuous enthusiasm. Instead of going to the Continent in the Spring she paid a visit to Ireland. There she approved the formation of the Irish Guards to mark the valour and sacrifice of her Irish soldiers in South Africa. She held receptions, gave Balls and reviewed troops and (on one occasion in Phoenix Park, Dublin, no less than 52,000) schoolchildren. While this visit went off very well, it is a sad fact that in all her reign the Queen spent only some five weeks in Ireland while she spent an aggregate of seven years in Scotland; the Irish did not forget. Later in the year she suffered more family bereavements with the death from cancer of the Duke of Edinburgh, her second son, in July and of Prince Christian Victor, her grandson, in October while on active service in South Africa. She knew too that her eldest daughter, the Empress Frederick of Prussia, was also dying of cancer. As the year came to its close there were rumours of her failing health and indeed, while not ill, she did not feel well, slept badly and ate little. On 22nd January 1901, the end came with little enough warning and she died in the early evening in the presence of her children and grandchildren, virtually supported so it is said, by His Imperial Majesty the Kaiser.

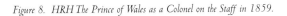

Figure 8. HRH The Prince of Wales as a Colonel on the Staff in 1859.

The Celebrations

Until 23rd September 1896, the reign of King George III had been the longest in English history. On that day, Queen Victoria overtook his record of fifty nine years and ninety-six days. But, when on 22nd June the following year, she achieved her Diamond Jubilee, it was not only a matter of personal and public satisfaction; it was also an opportunity for celebrations which were more extensive and surpassed in splendour any that had previously taken place in modern Europe.

The Queen's Golden Jubilee of 1887 had been a magnificent affair. But in the intervening ten years, much had happened. The Empire now covered a quarter of the earth's land mass, more than 11 million square miles; it was in fact 90 times greater in size than the Home country. Its peoples numbered some 400 million of nearly every race and culture. Politically it was a much stronger entity though paradoxically it had begun its process of dissolution. The immigrant people of Canada, the Australian States, New Zealand and The Cape had their own Parliaments which were all but completely independent of Westminster. If the legal ties were thus weakened, the bonds of loyalty to the Crown as the common focus became stronger. The people of these stronger Colonies, some now of Dominion status, saw Britain perfectly naturally as the mother country and the Queen equally naturally as their

Sovereign. Their loyalty and commitment to both was soon to be demonstrated by the willing despatch of troops to help Britain during the Anglo-Boer War of 1899-1902. And this spirit was again demonstrated in the present Century at much greater cost when men and women from all over the Empire joined with the British forces to fight Britain's enemies. But now, at the distance of a century, it is possible to see that the late 1890s probably marked the pinnacle of the prestige and power of the Empire which itself was the greatest in strength, extent and population size that the world has yet seen. It was held together not by force of occupation but by a rule of common law, by trade and by the Royal Navy. Within each territory, its own police and troops, supported only as necessary by the British Army, kept order and deterred or acted against external aggression. Where as in India a vast indigenous population was ruled by the British, power at a local level was in the hands of a tiny minority of Imperial civil servants and soldiers. They, in the vast majority of cases, were willingly obeyed; indeed, had this not been so, the system would have broken down. It never did break down. Its strength lay in the quality of such administrators who cheerfully shouldered their responsibility as much for (what we would now call) job satisfaction as for the hope of advancement. They in turn were controlled in career and political terms by a relatively small central British ruling leadership which had indeed already recognised that its days were numbered. It did not expect to leave India in the throes of the vast turbulence and horrific

Figure 9. Tuesday morning, 22nd June 1897 – Buckingham Palace Yard.

Figure 10. Jubilee Procession – Royal Naval Contingent in King William Street.

slaughter which eventually happened in 1947. But it did expect to go when the process of education and the rule of law had made it possible for Indians to carry on where they would leave off. How this might happen was of course in no way clear in 1897. India would be handed back one day; the so called "white" colonies would be handed over. The feeling about this was strong enough for the Prince of Wales, when King Edward VII and Emperor of India, to ponder whether he might indeed be the last of his line. But in the meantime, the Diamond Jubilee was an occasion which should be exploited for every ounce of political benefit which could be squeezed from it.

Detail planning began in February 1897. The basic idea of course was on the shelf and only needed to be dusted off: not only had the Golden Jubilee celebrations of 1887 been a great success but the principal players were still on the stage. The organising committee had been under the presidency of the Prince of Wales. Supported by Ministers, he had persuaded the Queen that a grand public display of the kind being considered would be a good idea. By nature shy, she had great difficulty in evading the easy option of hiding her public face behind her interminable mourning for the Prince Consort. Moreover she hated "fuss". But she was won over both politically and privately by the Imperial thrust of the occasion.

And so, while the Prince of Wales got on with the extensive and very complex arrangements, she was content to attend to the family issues involved. Not the least of these was the order of precedence with so many royal and titled guests. At any time this would have been a nightmare but on this occasion it was all settled very simply by the Queen's personal decision against which there could be no appeal!

Accession Day was 20th June. Nothing happened that day by the Queen's wish, out of respect for the memory of her uncle and predecessor, King William IV. For the following day, in 1887, a grand procession had been arranged to accompany the Queen to the climax of the celebrations, a Thanksgiving Service in Westminster Abbey. The Queen wore her customary, if expensive, mourning black. She refused to wear robes or a crown and persisted with her bonnet, a form of headgear which the ladies of the Court were instructed to wear as well. But if that bothered or disappointed her Ministers and ladies, it had little effect upon her public reception. In the Abbey with a congregation of thousands, she sat alone (hoping that she would not see Mr Gladstone who had been her Prime Minister three times and whom she could not abide); in her carriage, she sat with her daughter Victoria (Vicky), Crown Princess of Germany, and the Princess of Wales, and was seen by untold thousands of the public. What struck everyone was the animation of her face. Gone, it seemed, was the solemn mask of the last twenty-six years: quite plainly the Queen hugely enjoyed herself. She was cheered to the echo, evidence of her popularity which took her by surprise but much encouraged her. For the remaining thirteen years of her reign, she was in many ways rejuvenated in public even if she was in gently failing physical health and to many of her Household as daunting as ever.

In 1897, it was to be rather different and immeasurably grander. The Queen was in truth the grandmother of Europe and directly related to nearly every crowned head. As before she decided that she would not invite sovereigns and presidents but

Cathedral. Perhaps her carriage could be hauled bodily up the steps? Eventually, and happily, it was decided to hold the Service outside on the steps themselves so that the carriage could remain in the road and the Queen could take part without having to move from her seat. The second idea was even better: it was to extend the processional route over London Bridge and south of the River round to Westminster Bridge. Such a thing had never been done before and there was an immediate response from those poorer parts of the capital. Not only did people outdo themselves to cheer on the Queen, the Procession and anyone or anything else that took their fancy, but they were remarkably well behaved — to "the surprise and pleasure of the authorities". Admirable first aid

Figure 11. Jubilee Procession – Colonial Contingent moving south from London Bridge.

their heirs or representatives. It was again a family occasion but enhanced now by a world-wide recognition of her position which saw such incongruous neighbours in the Procession as the envoys of Hawaii and Korea riding on horseback together or the Chinese Ambassador sharing a carriage with the Papal Envoy. The planning had been meticulous from the order of precedence to the testing of the ramp by which the Queen would disembark from her train at Paddington. It was also complicated by two inspired ideas: the first was to have the Service of Thanksgiving at St Paul's thus making a distinction from the Coronation in Westminster Abbey. But as by now the Queen moved only with difficulty, the planners were confronted with the problem of how to convey her into the

arrangements had been made but were scarcely needed; not a single surgical case reached a hospital. But, surprising and happy as this was, the real gain was in the popularity of the monarch. It broke all bounds and remained so to the end of her reign.

The Queen's programme began with her arrival from Windsor by rail on the 21st. She was dressed in black as she had been daily since the death of the Prince Consort in 1861. Having driven in a carriage to Buckingham Palace, she was taken in her wheel chair to receive all the foreign royalty. Later she entertained them to dinner making her mark with a dress "of which the whole front was embroidered in gold, which had been specially worked in India, diamonds in my cap, and a diamond necklace..". She sat between the Prince of Naples, later King Victor Emmanuel III of Italy, and the Archduke Francis (or Franz) Ferdinand of Austria whose assassination in 1914 was to initiate the Great War and the end of the old order.

The next day, she was ensconced in her carriage ready to leave Buckingham Palace at 11.15 am. The day had begun watery and overcast but then, as though it had been ordered, the sun broke through at the very moment that the first gun signalling the Queen's departure went off in Hyde Park. It was soon noted that with her in the carriage were Princess Christian (of Schleswig-Holstein, the Queen's third daughter named Helena, nicknamed Lenchen) and the Princess of Wales (later Queen Alexandra). Sitting with their backs to the horses, they wore dresses in pale pastel shades. The Queen, facing them, had for once introduced a little relief to her usual strict mourning by wearing a black dress with panels of grey satin, though it was covered with black lace. Her black bonnet was trimmed with white flowers, a white aigrette and some black lace. She carried a pale grey silk parasol and very plainly enjoyed herself. She smiled and bowed to either side with, it was reported, special nods of recognition to courtiers and servants she spotted in the stands. Occasionally, so it seemed, she was on the verge of tears. But if she had wept not a soul would have blamed her for emotion charged the air. And so the vast procession which had been moving since soon after nine o'clock that morning brought the Queen to Temple Bar (then on Fleet Street) and the gates of the City of London. Here she

Figure 12. Jubilee Procession – Colonial troops from Hong Kong and Malaya in King William Street

Figure 13. Jubilee Procession – Pipe Band of the London Scottish passing the National Gallery.

stopped to be greeted by the Lord Mayor who presented to her and received back the pearl sword, a symbol of peaceful progress through the capital. That done, the Lord Mayor and the Sheriffs, on horseback, joined the procession and went ahead of the Queen as far as the Mansion House. And so, across Ludgate Circus and up the hill to St Paul's. The scene there has been well recorded by photograph but also in two splendid paintings: the steps crowded with the clerics in white and black and red. In the centre, the boys of the choir flanked by two great military bands, cavalry to the left and scarlet coated infantry to the right. Along the bottom step, members of the Honourable Corps of Gentlemen at Arms in scarlet coatees and gold lace, metal helmets with long white feather plumes; beyond them Yeomen of the Guard in their scarlet and gold tudor uniforms. In the very centre, the Archbishop of Canterbury and senior prelates in copes of many colours. Across the road, within the railings, were the members of the various princely escorts in their multi-coloured uniforms.

Outside the railings the carriages of the Royal Family were parked in order, their occupants standing up, the younger ones in great excitement, to see what was going on. Further back around the Churchyard, the members of the Colonial military contingents who had arrived more than an hour before, were mostly able to see the Queen, and would hear it all. When at last the tableau froze, it was with the Queen in the centre, her sons and the Duke of Cambridge opposite her, Lord Wolseley before her and Lord Roberts behind her. Truly it was an Army day (though the Royal Navy would have their turn later). The cheers were hushed as the choir and the bands launched into the Te Deum; the Lord's Prayer was chanted, the Bishop of London said a special Jubilee prayer and the Archbishop of Canterbury gave the Benediction. There followed the old 100th Psalm "All people that on earth do dwell" sung by thousands in the area and it was time to move. But then, in a movement which seems to have been entirely spontaneous, the people interfered in the planning and as if by common consent

18

Figure 14. Jubilee Procession — Equerries and Suites in Cheapside.

began to sing the National Anthem. The dense crowds lining the streets to the east, west and south took up the air so that it seemed that the whole of London was in voice. The effect was stupendous. The Archbishop of Canterbury, gripped by the excitement of the moment, so far forgot his clerical dignity as to call for three cheers for the Queen! And the people responded in explosion after explosion of sound reverberating like the roll of thunder far into the distance.

On then to the Mansion House where the Queen's carriage paused once more to enable her to receive a silver basket of orchids from the Lady Mayoress and to say farewell to the Lord Mayor. On again through streets which to the now tired Queen must have begun to seem endless until eventually, at 1.45 pm she arrived back at Buckingham Palace. After a quiet lunch, there was time for a rest before a large dinner from which she felt able to retire at 11 pm. The processional route had been more than six miles. The procession was composed of some 3500 people, its route was lined by an estimated 20,000 soldiers, and the day's proceedings were watched at first hand by countless thousands; only the two bridges were devoid of spectators who otherwise crowded stands and windows or stood up to ten deep on the pavements. As the end of the Procession passed along the streets, so the crowd spread into

the road behind it. The spectators formed a broad, densely packed and slowly moving river of humanity, more than sufficient in the words of one observer "to have populated the whole of Great Britain in the days of Shakespeare". And for hours this human river flowed on, increasing rather than diminishing in volume for tributaries flowed in from every side street along the way. So vast was the multitude that no police could have controlled it. But it did not want controlling. It was not a mob but an amazingly self-disciplined host. It was light-hearted and merry, it sang and it danced, it laughed and it shouted; but whatever it did the rough element seemed to have been smoothed out of it that Jubilee night. And what a night it was. The main streets of the capital were illuminated in a fairyland of festoons and garlands the extent of which had never been seen before. Nor were these demonstrations confined to London for across the country two thousand bonfires blazed on hills and every town and village "had its own miniature celebration". Nor was this confined to Home for across the Empire every City and town showed its loyalty in a myriad ways — except only India which was preoccupied with plague in Bombay, earthquake in Calcutta and the smouldering beginnings of the Great Rising along the Frontier to the North West. But for London, as the article (which follows) by GW

Figure 15. Jubilee Procession — Lord Roberts (centre) in front of St Paul's, with Colonial troops and Foot Guards behind, watches the Procession.

Figure 16. Jubilee Procession — Officers of Indian State Forces in King William Street.

Figure 17. Jubilee Procession – Indian Cavalry Officers in King William Street; Lord Wolseley and then the Queen's carriage just behind.

Steevens so graphically illustrates, the 22nd June 1897 had been the greatest, most colourful, exciting, emotional, powerful and happy State occasion in perfect weather that had ever happened before or indeed was probably ever to happen again.

But it did not end there. The next afternoon, the Queen received the Lords and the Commons, some 700 of them, in the Ballroom of Buckingham Palace. Each House was to present an Address of Congratulation to which the Queen would return a "gracious Answer". When it came to the turn of the House of Commons, there was something of a breakdown in what should of course have been a carefully planned and well orchestrated event. With the Queen and her suite established at one end of the room, the doors at the other were flung open. In came the Commons "like a crowd being let onto the ground after a football match. There seemed to be no order and the Speaker, Prime Minister and Leader of the Opposition were lost in the struggling mass of MPs. This dishevelled mass of humanity came at the Queen and instinctively the men of the Household felt that they were called upon to do or die." While order was restored, they formed a a protective screen around the Queen. She was thoroughly put out and did not mince her words to the Lord Chamberlain and the Lord Steward, the two officials of the Household between whom this most unfortunate affair had

slipped without either of them exercising effective control. After some 15 minutes the Queen had had enough and withdrew. But, recognising that the members of the two Houses were just as much victims as she was herself, she gave a garden party ten days later for them all with their wives and daughters. Later that Wednesday, 23rd June, the Queen left Buckingham Palace via an inspection of the Yeomen of the Guard drawn up in the Palace garden, and a concourse of schoolchildren in the stands for the Jubilee Procession on Constitution Hill. The crowds on the pavements were at least as dense as the day before. From Paddington she travelled by rail to Slough and then went in a carriage procession with a mounted escort via Eton College and past no less than four Guards of Honour to Windsor Castle. The evening was quiet; all the Queen's royal and representational guests were treated to a State Opera performance at Covent Garden hosted in her absence by the Prince and Princess of Wales. On Thursday, the Queen received Naval officers of foreign countries whose ships were visiting for the forthcoming Naval Review and on Friday she inspected representative detachments of Fire Brigades from all over the country. On Saturday 26th June, the great Naval Review took place at Spithead while the Queen, one assumes from an absence of report, had a rest from her efforts.

The Royal Navy had not fought a pitched battle at sea

Figure 18. Jubilee Procession – The Queen in Piccadilly.

Figure 19. Jubilee Procession – The Queen in Cheapside, cheered by the boys of Christ's Hospital.

Figure 20. Jubilee Procession – The Queen at the Mansion House.

Figure 21 Jubilee Review at Aldershot, 1st July 1897. Massed mounted bands (of, from left, 1st Life Guards, 6th Dragoon Guards, Royal Dragoons, 12th Lancers and Royal Artillery) pass the Queen.

against an enemy fleet since the Battle of Trafalgar almost 92 years before. It had not needed to for although the Army was extensively engaged throughout the century there had been no attack against the Home country. The closest to active service by a fleet had been the Bombardments of Acre in 1840 and of Alexandria in 1882. But neither could be called a battle. It could be said, therefore, that the Royal Navy had deterred war

and thus preserved peace. Plainly, so thought the Special Ambassador of the United States when, gazing at the assembled naval might, he remarked to the First Lord of the Admiralty: "I guess, Sir, this makes for peace." The statistics were impressive: one hundred and seventy three warships, including 21 Battleships and 53 Cruisers, manned by some 38,000 sailors had been brought together without, it was said,

Figure 22. Jubilee Review at Aldershot. Colonial Cavalry, Canadians in the front rank followed by Australians.

Figure 23. Review of Colonial Contingents at Windsor, 2nd July 1897. From the left, Hong Kong Regiment, Canadian Infantry, British Guiana Constabulary.

Figure 24. Review of Colonial Contingents at Windsor, 2nd July 1897. From the left, in the foreground an officer of the Royal Malta Artillery; in line, Chinese Submarine Mine Engineers from Hong Kong, Singapore Engineers, West Indies Royal Enginers, Mauritius Enginers, Malta Submarine Mine Engineers, Hong Kong Artillery and Mauritius Royal Artillery with officer in front.

weakening naval strength in the Mediterranean, the China Station, in African and Indian waters, in the Pacific and off Australasia, nor in the Atlantic. This gigantic display of warlike force brought together for the purpose of jubilation was arranged in four lines stretching over 30 miles between Bembridge Point and the coast at Cowes. At two o'clock, the Prince of Wales and his family aboard the Royal Yacht set off to steam down the lines of ships and to be deafened by gun salutes as they went. He had given orders that the crews were not to cheer but as these had no effect on countless private vessels nor on foreign warships, his progress was accompanied

by roars of acclamation. Not to be outdone, the Royal Navy joined in. At 3 pm, the Prince of Wales anchored and invited all the Admirals to tea on the Royal Yacht the better to congratulate and thank them for the efforts of the Fleet. Its presentation had impressed not only the home watchers on the shore but much more importantly the many foreign observers, and had thus enhanced the prestige and power of the Empire. In the evening, the Prince of Wales steamed out once again to the Fleet whichwas now dressed overall in electric lights enhanced by impromptu fireworks displays from the foreign ships. And so it was, appropriately enough, that the public part

Figure 25. Review of the Colonial Contingents at Windsor, 2nd July 1897. From the left, Royal Niger Haussas, Sierra Leone Frontier Force, Lagos Constabulary.

Figure 26. Review of the Colonial Contingents at Windsor, 2nd July 1897. From the left, Hong Kong Regiment with officer, Canadian Infantry with Major of 2nd Rifles in front.

of the Diamond Jubilee celebrations was concluded by a mighty seafaring nation on the sea.

For the Queen herself, it was not quite over yet. On Thursday 1st July, she travelled from Windsor to Aldershot to review the Colonial forces in England for the Jubilee together with Regular troops of the Aldershot District and Militia troops under training. Under the command of General HRH The Duke of Connaught and Strathearn, the Home forces present consisted of seven Regiments of Cavalry, nine Batteries of the Royal Artillery, four Field Companies and specialist elements of the Royal Engineers, and no less than 34 Battalions of Infantry. It was a remarkable show not only for the very large number of soldiers gathered together in one place but also for the presence of all seven battalions of Foot Guards. The latter had not assembled since they were reviewed by the Queen and the Prince Consort in Hyde Park on their return from the Crimea in 1856.

On Friday 2nd July, the Queen reviewed the Colonial contingent's in Windsor Home Park in order to thank them for coming and to wish them a safe journey home. And finally on Monday 5th July, the Indian contingents were assembled on the East Lawn of Windsor Castle and greeted the Queen with a series of mounted and then dismounted evolutions. Each

Indian officer received the Jubilee Commemoration Medal and the military element of the Jubilee was thus brought to an end. The political and Court functions went on for another fortnight so that it was not until 20th July when she left for Osborne House on the Isle of Wight that the Jubilee could be said to be over.

Looking back especially to the Procession on 22nd June, there is no doubt at all that it was an enormous success. Immaculate planning coupled with the favour of "Queen's weather" had produced an immaculate spectacle. Plain also was the symbolism. Foreign envoys were impressed: from Washington to Korea and from Hawaii to St Petersburg, the nations of the world delivered their messages of friendship – and took away their interpretation of what it all meant. The ability of the Crown to make and cement friendships was endorsed as never before, a movement which the Prince of Wales made his own from the day he ascended the throne as King Edward VII. It is hard now to view these events without seeing the tragedy of 1914 hanging like a gathering storm over them. But at the time, with seventeen years yet to go, it would have been hard for anyone with a rational and objective view of affairs to see the Jubilee as anything other than a vast and powerful act of peaceable celebration.

Figure 27. Review of the Colonial Contingents at Windsor, 2nd July 1897. From the left, Ceylon Light Infantry, North Borneo Police, British, Indian and Chinese Police of Hong Kong, Gold Coast Haussas, Royal Niger Haussas.

Report of the Correspondent of The Daily Mail

The Queen's Procession has passed. It is over, and we are all the richer and all the better for it. We have seen a sight the like of which no eye has seen since the world began. We do not know whether we want to laugh or to cry. But how proud, how proud we all mst be today.

At St Paul's it began like any other show. We were boxed up between the pillars and the wall in a little cage of carpentry. There were pillars in front of us, and I doubt if people quite realise the massive stability of the pillars in the portico of St Paul's until in the exercise of their professoional duty they are called upon to see through them. There were also beams across the pillars, and across the line of sight. But never mind all that: we could see down Ludgate Hill. And Ludgate Hill Was bedecked and bedraped as I never saw any street before in London or anywhere else. Pale purple, pale gold, and pale green – masts and hanging brackets and swinging garlands – a long, drooping vista of pillars and capitals and festoons, all softly harmonious. Any decoration can make a street brilliant if there is enough of it, but Ludgate Hill was beautiful. It was quite transformed from the sooty, busy, Ludgate Hill of work days. Under the still shy, half watery, sunlight it dipped down to the railway bridge; this also flagged and flowered for the great day, with two girls in white in the centre for a focus; and then sloped up through the Circus to Fleet Street, with the turret of Lincolns Inn Hall crowning the distance. It was all a sheen with a mellow radiance still enough for dignity, but yet shimmering with life. For the chief of all the decorations were the masses of swaying white and pink in the windows, lining every house from foundation to topmost storey and massed on every roof. London had decorated itself with Londoners, and

Figure 28. Jubilee Procession – The Queen at St Paul's.

with men and women from every part of England and every inch of ther world where people stand up for "God Save the Queen".

It began like any other show, with a maze of gay-coloured women looking for their seats, with foot guards marching through the barrier to the top of Ludgate Hill and lining up along the churchyard pavement. There were the ponderous vans labelled "City Commissioner of Sewers" lumbering between the banks of colour, as if the Empire had turned out to see them scatter sand. Then the place cleared; the last summer gown fluttered to its own place; the scarlet guardsmen were all in position; the last sandcart lumbered away eastward. All was ready; we waited for it to begin.

It began as it should begin with the Fleet. Swinging and dancing up the Hill came the tilted straw hats of the naval guard of honour. The fifes screamed out "They All Love Jack". And how they do love Jack; how the hill and the churchyard thundered! And how worthy Jack is to be loved. Clean limbs, strong bodies, trim, alert, resourceful, self-reliant, their buoyant march quivered with young life; their eyes were set with the steadfast calm of men who have been left alone with God's wonders at sea. Beside them marched their bearded captains and lieutenants, quiet, self-possessed, intent on the business they know and love; and their middies, pink-faced boys, already men in self-command and the habit of commanding others. There was good marching after that, but no marching so elastic as this. The sight of that magnificent guard was worth the whole day's preparations in itself. We felt we could never go wrong with these men. And how good to feel that we were showing them to the representatives of every nation on earth — showing them the finest force in the whole world.

They formed up and we waited again. Another clash of music from beyond the railway bridge, and we were looking at what all England was longing to look at — the colonials. But first a scarlet plumed figure on a white horse pacing up the street, and all the street breaking into a roar as he came up. Roberts! Three cheers for Roberts! Bobs, Bobs, Bobs! What a proud and beautiful horse, that hardly felt the ground it trod on, and what a man! Hard-bitten, tanned face, the white moustache sitting firmly on the firm mouth, bolt upright yet easy in the saddle — Lord Roberts was every inch a soldier and captain of men. When Sir Charles Napier first heard Braham sing he went up to him and said, "Sir, it is men like you that make men like we". It is men like Lord Roberts that make queens like Queen Victoria.

The cheers sank, but they did not die, for before there was time for that we were looking at the colonials. In the carriages we saw the square, strong, invincibly sensible faces of the men who are building up great nations, new big Englands, on the other side of the world. Between the carriages rode and tramped the men who guard the building, and who carry British peace and British law into the wildest places of this earth. Lean, hard-knit, Canadians, long-legged yellow Australians, all in one piece with their horses, giant, long-eyed Maoris, sitting loosely and leaning back curiously from the waist; burned South Africans; upstanding Sikhs, tiny lithe Malays and Dyaks;

Chinese with a white basin turned upside-down on their heads; grinning Hausas, so dead black that they shone silver in the sun — white men, yellow men, brown men, black men, every colour, every continent, every race, every speech — and all in arms for the British Empire and the British Queen. Up they came, more and more, new types, new realms at every couple of yards, an anthropological museum — a living gazeteer of the British Empire. With them came their English officers, whom they obey and follow like children. And you began to understand, as never before, what the Empire amounts to. Not only that we possess all these remote outlandish places, and can bring men from every end of the earth to join us in honouring our Queen, but also that all these people are working, not simply under us, but with us — that we send out a boy here and a boy there, and the boy takes hold of the savages of the part he comes to, and teaches them to march and shoot as he tells them, to obey him and believe in him and die for him and the Queen. A plain, stupid, uninspired, people they call us, and yet we are doing this with every kind of savage man there is. And each one of us — you and I, and that man in his shirt-sleeves at the corner — is a working part of this world-shaping force. How small you must feel in face of the stupendous whole, and yet how great to be a unit in it!

The British Empire fell in along the pavement, at the top of Ludgate Hill, and round the churchyard, and there waited. Presently there was another stir and bustle at the bottom of the hill, and another burst of brass. There came into sight under the bridge and up the hill a moving wall of men and horses. First more bluejackets, trailing their guns behind them, hauling on to the ropes so steadily and evenly that the guns seemed to be alive and walking of themselves. Then cavalry and guns — now massed bands crashing out music, now serried squadrons, now gliding horse-batteries. They came like a wall, as close, as perfectly even, and level and smooth; the squadrons looked as if they had been put together with a spirit-level and trimmed with a plane. The approach to the Cathedral was a blaze of blue and scarlet; the sun on swords and helmets laced the blue and scarlet with gold. The eye was filled with splendour, but fresh splendour came crowding in on it. The advancing pageant shifted and loosened and came up in opener order. But as the mass of colour became less massive it became more wonderfully coloured. Here, riding three and three, came a kaleidoscope of dazzling horsemen — equerries and aides-de-camp and attaches, ambassadors and princes, all the pomp of all the nations of the earth. Scarlet and gold, azure and gold, purple and gold, emerald and gold, white and gold — always a changing tumult of colours that seemed to list and gleam with a light of their own, and always blinding gold. It was enough. No eye could bear more gorgeousness; no more gorgeousness could be, unless princes are to clothe themselves in rainbows and the very sun. The prelude was played, and now the great moment was at hand. Already the carriages were rolling up full of the Queen's kindred, full of her children and children's children. But we hardly looked at them. Down there, through an avenue of eager faces, through a storm of white waving handkerchiefs, through roaring volleys of cheers, there was approaching a carriage drawn by eight cream-coloured horses. The roar surged up the street, keeping pace with the eight horses. The carriage passed the barrier; it entered the churchyard; it wheeled left and then right; it drew up at the very steps of the Cathedral; we all leaped up; cheers broke into screams, and enthusiasm swelled to delirium; the sun, watery till now, shone out suddenly clear and dry, and there – and there -

And there was a little, plain, flushed old lady. All in black, a silver streak under the black bonnet, a simple white sunshade, sitting quite still, with the corners of her mouth drawn tight, as if she were trying not to cry. But that old lady was the Queen, and you knew it. You didn't want to look at the glittering uniforms now, nor yet at the bright gowns and the young faces in the carriages, nor yet at the stately princes – though by now all these were ranged in a half circle around her. You couldn't look at anybody but the Queen. So very quiet, so very grave, so very punctual, so unmistakeably and every inch a lady and a Queen. Almost pathetic, if you will, that small black figure in the middle of these shining cavaliers, this great army, this roaring multitude; but also very glorious. When the other kings of the world drive abroad, the escort rides close in at the wheels of the carriage; the Queen drove through her people quite plain and open, with just one soldier at the kerbstone between her and them. Why not? They are quite free; they have no cause to fear her; they have much cause to love her. Was it not all for her – the gala trappings of the streets, the men and horses and guns, the living walls of British men and women? For the Queen summed up all that had gone before, all the soldiers and sailors, the big-limbed colonial, the strange men from unheard-of islands oversea. We know now what that which had come before all stood for; we knew as we had never known before what the Queen stands for. The Empire had come together to revere and bless the mother of the Empire.

The mother of the Empire had come to do homage to the one Being more majestic than she. There are the archbishops and the bishops and the deans in gold and crimson caps and white and orange and gold-embroidered vestments, waiting on the steps. There, through the gaps in the pillars and scaffoldings, you could see all her Ministers and great men – a strange glimpse of miniature faces as in some carefully laboured picture where each face stands for an honoured name. All stood, and the choir sang the Te Deum. The Queen put on her glasses and looked gravely at the shoal of grave faces. Next rose up a melodious voice intoning prayers. The Queen bowed her head. Then the whole choir and company outside the Cathedral and the whole company in the stands and at the windows and on the housetops and away down the street, all standing, all uncovered, began to sing the Hundredth Psalm. "Come ye before Him and rejoice": the Queen's lips were tight, and her eyes – perhaps it was fancy – looked dim. But then "Three cheers for the Queen!" and the dean – pious man – was wildly waving that wonderful crimson cap, and the pillars and roofs were ringing as if they must come down. Then "God Save the Queen" – a lusty peal till you felt drowned in sound. The Queen looked up and smiled. And the Queen's smile was the end and crown of it all. A smile that broke down the sad

mouth, a smile that seemed half-reluctant – so wistful, yet so kind, so sincere, so motherly.

God Save the Queen!

G W Steevens

Editorial Note:

G W Steevens was one of that breed of Victorian newspaper people who informed. They may have criticised where criticism was due but above all they gave information, as well as pleasure. In an age when much happened and the public thirst for knowledge was great, the logic of this was clear. It is a matter for regret that nowadays all newspapers appear to find it more important and rewarding to sensationalise than to inform. G W Steevens wrote not just for newspapers but also for publishers of books. He is well known today for his classic account of Kitchener's 1898 campaign in the Sudan. The book is titled in good Henty style "With Kitchener to Khartum (sic)" and it is an excellent read. The following year he was off to South Africa where he produced another volume in a similar form. But, tragically, he also found his grave. He died of fever on 15th January 1900.

Figure 29. Field Marshal Lord Roberts of Kandahar mounted on Vonolel, 1897.

Appendix 1

The Procession to St Paul's

TUESDAY 22ND JUNE 1897

The purpose of the Procession was to escort the Queen to St Paul's for a Service of Thanksgiving and to enable her to see her people and to receive their congratulations on having attained the Sixtieth Anniversary of her accession. It was also to demonstrate in a political sense the extent, world-wide scope and power of the British Empire.

The Procession began from Buckingham Palace, went up Constitution Hill, right along Piccadilly, right down St James's Street, left along Pall Mall, along the north side of Trafalgar Square, the Strand, Fleet Street, across Ludgate Circus and up Ludgate Hill to St Paul's. Here a Service was conducted in the open, the Queen remaining in her carriage at the foot of the steps. The Procession then moved by the south side of St Paul's along Cheapside to the Mansion House. From there it went down King William Street, over London Bridge and through Borough High Street, along Borough Road, over St George's Circus, up Westminster Bridge Road to Westminster Bridge, past Big Ben turning right into Whitehall; it turned left to pass through the Horse Guards Arch and then followed the route taken annually to this day by the Queen's Birthday Parade up the Mall and so to Buckingham Palace.

The troops on parade may be divided into three groups:

✡ The street lining parties (not listed here).

✡ The Colonial Procession, which preceded the Queen's Procession on the route to St Paul's. After the service of Thanksgiving, it followed a short distance behind the Queen's Procession on the route back to Buckingham Palace.

✡ The Queen's Procession, which left Buckingham Palace at 11.15 am.

In this part, we list the naval, military and Royal components of the two Processions.

Figure 30. Canadian Contingent to the Jubilee Celebrations in England.

The Colonial Procession

(MOUNTED PORTION)

Advanced party Royal Horse Guards (four men)

Band of the Royal Horse Guards

Field Marshal The Right Hon Lord Roberts of Kandahar KP GCB GCSI GCIE VC, Commanding Colonial Troops

Colonel Ivor Herbert CB CMG, Grenadier Guards

Detachment Royal Canadian Dragoons (Regular Force)

Detachments of Canadian Cavalry Regiments (Militia Force) (see Note A)

Detachment North West Mounted Police of Canada

Detachment New South Wales Lancers

Detachment New South Wales Mounted Rifles

Detachment Victoria Mounted Rifles

Detachment New Zealand Mounted Rifles

Detachment South Australian Mounted Rifles

Detachment Queensland Mounted Rifles

Detachment Cape Mounted Rifles

Detachment Natal Carbineers

Detachment Umvoti Mounted Rifles

Detachment Natal Mounted Rifles

Detachment Border Mounted Rifles

Detachment Ceylon Mounted Infantry

Detachment Trinidad Yeomanry (or Trinidad Light Horse)

Detachment Cyprus Military Police (or Zaptiehs)

Detachment Rhodesian Horse

(DISMOUNTED PORTION)

Band of the 1st Middlesex (Victoria and St George's) Rifle Volunteers

Detachment Royal Malta Regiment of Militia

Detachment Royal Malta Artillery

Detachment Royal Canadian Artillery

Detachment Trinidad Field Artillery Volunteers

Detachment Trinidad Light Infantry Volunteers

Detachment Trinidad Police

Detachment Kingston Garrison Artillery, Jamaica Militia

Detachment Kingston Infantry, Jamaica Militia

Detachment Bermuda Militia Artillery

Detachment St Lucia Artillery

Detachment of Perth Artillery Volunteers (Western Australia Volunteer Force)

Figure 31. Troop Sergeant Major, Governor General's Bodyguard, Canada.

Figure 32. Canadian Cavalry officers and soldiers (for detail, see Appendix 4).

Detachments of Infantry (Western Australia Volunteer Force)

Detachment Hong Kong Engineers (Submarine Miners)

Detachments of the Malay States Guides

Detachment of Malay Police

Detachment Singapore Royal Enginers (Volunteers)

Detachment West Indies Royal Engineers (Volunteers)

Detachment Mauritius Royal Engineers

Detachment Malta Militia Division Submarine Miners, Royal Engineers

Detachment Hong Kong Garrison Artillery

Detachment Mauritius Royal Artillery

Detachment Ceylon Royal Engineers

Detachment New South Wales Field Artillery

Detachment New South Wales Garrison Artillery

Detachment New South Wales Engineers

Pipe Band of the London Scottish Rifle Volunteers

Detachment 2nd West India Regiment

Detachment Hong Kong Regiment

Detachment Royal Canadian Infantry Regiment (Permanent Force)

Detachments of Regiments of Canadian Militia Infantry (see Note B)

Detachment of British Guiana Constabulary

Detachment Ceylon Garrison Artillery

Detachment Ceylon Light Infantry Volunteers

Detachment British North Borneo Dyak Police

Detachments of European, Sikh and Chinese Police of Hong Kong

Band of the London Irish Rifle Volunteer Corps

Detachment Gold Coast Hausa Constabulary

Detachment Royal Niger Company (Hausa) Constabulary

Detachment Sierra Leone Frontier Police

Detachment Lagos (Hausa) Constabulary

Mounted Detachment Canadian Cavalry

The Queen's Procession

Captain O Ames, 2nd Life Guards

Four troopers, 2nd Life Guards

Detachment Royal Navy with six guns

Staff Officer

Advance Guard, 2nd Life Guards

(Royal Horse Artillery and Cavalry)

Royal Artillery Mounted Band

D Battery Royal Horse Artillery

Mounted Bands of 1st Life Guards, 1st (King's) Dragoon Guards and 2nd Dragoon Guards (Queen's Bays)

Squadron, 1st Life Guards

Squadron, 1st (King's) Dragoon Guards

Figure 33. New South Wales Lancers.

Squadron, 2nd Dragoon Guards (Queen's Bays)

E Battery Royal Horse Artillery

Mounted Bands of 3rd (Prince of Wales's) Dragoon Guards,
6th Dragoon Guards (Carabiniers)
and 7th (Princess Royal's) Dragoon Guards

Squadron, 3rd (Prince of Wales's) Dragoon Guards

Squadron, 6th Dragoon Guards (Carabiniers)

Squadron, 7th (Princess Royal's) Dragoon Guards

G Battery Royal Horse Artillery

Mounted Bands of 1st (Royal) Dragoons, 2nd Dragoons
(Royal Scots Greys) and 6th (Inniskilling) Dragoons

Squadron, 1st (Royal) Dragoons

Squadron, 2nd Dragoons (Royal Scots Greys)

Squadron, 6th (Inniskilling) Dragoons

J Battery Royal Horse Artillery

Mounted Bands of 3rd (King's Own) Hussars and 8th
(King's Royal Irish) Hussars

Squadron, 3rd (King's Own) Hussars

Squadron, 8th (King's Royal Irish) Hussars

O Battery Royal Horse Artillery

Mounted Bands of 10th (Prince of Wales's Own Royal)
Hussars and 15th (The King's) Hussars

Squadron, 10th (Prince of Wales's Own Royal) Hussars

Squadron, 15th (The King's) Hussars

T Battery Royal Horse Artillery

Mounted Bands of 12th (Prince of Wales's Royal) Lancers
and 17th (Duke of Cambridge's Own) Lancers

Squadron, 12th (Prince of Wales's Royal) Lancers

Squadron, 17th (Duke of Cambridge's Own) Lancers

P Battery Royal Horse Artillery

(The Aides-de-Camp to the Commander-in-Chief)

Figure 34. New South Wales Mounted Rifles

Brevet Colonel The Earl of Erroll
Major The Hon W Coke, Rifle Brigade
Captain A A Weldon, 4th Battalion Leinster Regiment
Brevet Lieutenant Colonel J Adye, Royal Artillery

(Military Aides-de-Camp to the Queen)

Colonel R MacG Stewart CB
Brevet Colonel R Garnett CB

(Naval Aides-de-Camp to the Queen)

Admiral Sir Algernon McL Lyons KCB
Captain E Neville Rolfe CB RN
Captain A W Moore CMG RN
Captain W A D Acland RN
Captain Lord Charles Beresford CB RN
Captain J H Bainbridge RN
Colonel W Campbell, Royal Marine Artillery
Colonel A B Crosbie, Royal Marines Light Infantry

*Figure 35. Colonel H B Lassetter of the New South Wales Mounted Rifles who
commanded the Colonial Escort in the Procession.*

(Militia Aides-de-Camp to the Queen)

Colonel The Right Hon The Earl of Derby GCB, 3rd
Battalion Royal Lancaster Regiment
Colonel The Right Hon Lord Suffield KCB, Norfolk
Artillery (Eastern Division Royal Artillery)
Colonel The Right Hon The Earl Percy,
3rd Battalion Northumberland Fusiliers
Colonel Sir R H A Ogilvy, Bart, Forfar and Kincardine
Artillery (Southern Division Royal Artillery)
Colonel J Davis, 3rd Battalion Royal West Surrey Regiment
Colonel The Earl of March, 3rd Battalion Royal Sussex
Regiment

(Yeomanry Aides-de-Camp to the Queen)

Colonel The Right Hon The Earl of Cork and Orrery KP,
North Somerset Yeomanry Cavalry
Colonel The Earl of Haddington, Lothian and Berwick
Yeomanry Cavalry
Colonel The Right Hon Lord Belper, late Nottinghamshire
Yeomanry Cavalry

(Volunteers Aides-de-Camp to the Queen)

Colonel The Earl of Wemyss,
7th Middlesex Volunteer Rifle Corps
Colonel Lord Blythswood,
3rd Volunteer Battalion Highland Light Infantry
Colonel B G D Cooke,
2nd Volunteer Battalion Royal Welsh Fusiliers
Colonel J Stevenson, 9th Lanark Volunteer Rifle Corps
Colonel J H Rivett-Carnac CIE, Commandant
4th Administrative Battalion North West Province
of India Volunteers

(The Lord Lieutenant of London)

The Duke of Westminster KG

Figure 36. Victoria Mounted Rifles.

(The Headquarters Staff of the Army)

Colonel The Hon G H Gough CB,
Private Secretary to the Commander-in-Chief
Major General C Grove CB,
Military Secretary
Major General M Protheroe CB CSI, Assistant Military
Secretary (for Indian Affairs)

General The Right Hon Sir R Buller GCB KCMG VC,
Adjutant-General to the Forces
Major General C F Clery CB,
Deputy Adjutant-General to the Forces
Colonel R E Allen, Assistant Adjutant-General
Major F R C Carleton,
Deputy-Assistant Adjutant-General
Brevet Major F Hammersley,
Deputy-Assistant Adjutant-General
Captain F S Robb, Deputy-Assistant Adjutant-General
Major General Sir F W Grenfell GCMG KCB,
Inspector-General of Auxiliary Forces and Recruiting
Major General F T Lloyd CB, Deputy Adjutant-General,
Royal Artillery
Colonel A E Turner CB, Assistant Adjutant-General,
Royal Artillery
Major F G Stone, Deputy-Assistant Adjutant-General,
Royal Artillery
Major General W Salmond CB,
Assistant Adjutant-General, Royal Engineers
Colonel D A Scott DSO,
Assistant Adjutant-General, Royal Engineers
General Sir H Evelyn Wood GCB GCMG VC,
Quartermaster-General to the Forces
Colonel A G Raper, Assistant Quartermaster-General
Major H M Lawson, Deputy-Assistant Quartermaster-
General
Lieutenant General Sir R Grant KCB,
Inspector-General of Fortifications
Lieutenant General E Markham,
Inspector-General of Ordnance
Colonel R A Montgomery,
Deputy Inspector-General of Ordnance
Surgeon Major General J Jameson MD, Director-General
Army Medical Department
Veterinary Colonel J D Lambert CB,
Director-General Army Veterinary Department

Representatives of Colonial Forces in England for the Diamond Jubilee, 1897

KEY TO FIGURE 37 (Previous page)

1. Garrison Artillery (Canada)
2. Malay States Guide
3. Malay Police
4. British Guiana Police
5. Trinidad Light Infantry
6. Garrison Artillery (Mauritius) Sikhs
7. Ceylon Infantry Volunteers
8. New South Wales Engineers
9. Ceylon Engineers
10. Canada Field Artillery
11. Royal Regiment Canadian Infantry
12. Royal Engineers (Mauritius)
13. Ceylon Artillery Volunteers
14. Gold Coast Constabulary (Haussas)
15. Hong Kong Garrison Artillery (Sikhs)
16. West Indian Royal Engineers
17. West Australia (Perth) Artillery Volunteers
18. Singapore Royal Engineers
19. 68th Regiment (Canada)
20. West Australia 1st Infantry Volunteers
21. 62nd Fusileers (St Johns, Canada)
22. 2nd Queen's Own Rifles (Canada)
23. Governor-General's Foot-Guards (Canada)
24. European Police (Hong Kong)
25. West Indian Regiment
26. Sierra Leone Frontier Force
27. Royal Malta Engineers
28. Royal Grenadiers (Toronto, Canada)
29. Trinidad Field Artillery
30. Princess of Wales's Own Rifles (Canada)
31. Bermuda Militia Artillery
32. 48th Highlanders (Canada)
33. Jamaica Militia
34. Hong Kong Sikh Police
35. Royal Malta Militia
36. Trinidad Police
37. New South Wales Field Artillery
38. Lagos Haussas
39. South Australian Mounted Rifles
40. North West Police (Canada)
41. Victoria Mounted Rifles
42. Governor-General's Bodyguard (Canada)
43. Royal Canadian Dragoons
44. Rhodesian Horse
45. Cape Mounted Rifles
46. New South Wales Lancers
47. New Zealand Mounted Rifles
48. 1st Central India Horse
49. Queensland Mounted Rifles
50. 10th Bengal Lancers
51. King's Own Hussars (Canada)
52. Trinidad Light Horse
53. 17th Bengal Cavalry
54. Ceylon Mounted Infantry
55. New South Wales Mounted Rifles
56. 5th Bengal Cavalry
57. 3rd Lancers (Hyderabad Contingent)
58. Cyprus Mounted Police
59. Royal Malta Artillery
60. Subadar, 1st Madras Lancers
61. 5th Punjab Cavalry
62. 3rd Prince of Wales's Dragoon Guards (Canada)
63. Bombay Lancers, 1 D.C.O.
64. 13th Bengal Lancers
65. 7th Bombay Lancers
66. 1st Hussars (Canada)
67. 16th Bengal Lancers
68. Natal Carbineers
69. 7th Bengal Lancers
70. North Borneo Police
71. Hong Kong Chinese Police
72. Manitoba Dragoons (Canada)
73. Jamaica Artillery
74. Hong Kong Regiment
75. Hong Kong Engineers
76. St. Lucia Artillery
77. Royal Niger Haussas
78. Viceroy of India's Bodyguard
79. New South Wales Garrison Artillery
80. 12th Bengal Cavalry
81. 2nd Bengal Lancers
82. 6th Bombay Cavalry
83. 4th Bengal Cavalry
84. Sierra Leone Royal Artillery
85. 8th Bengal Cavalry
86. 3rd Bengal Cavalry
87. 9th Bengal Lancers
88. 5th Bombay Cavalry
89. 2nd Lancers (Hyderabad Contingent)

(Field Marshals)

Field Marshal Sir Lintorn Simmons GCB GCMG   Field Marshal Sir Donald Stewart, Bart,GCB GCSI CIE

(Three officers representing the Auxiliary Force in attendance on HRH The Prince of Wales)

Colonel Viscount Coke,
Commanding Prince of Wales' Own
Norfolk Artillery,
representing the Militia

Lieutenant Colonel The Earl of
Albemarle, Commanding Civil
Service Volunteers
representing the Volunteers

Lieutenant Colonel Viscount Valentia,
Commanding Queen's Own
Oxfordshire Hussars
representing the Yeomanry

(Suites, Equerries and Gentlemen in attendance, riding in threes)

Colonel C Swaine
In attendance on HRH The Duke
Albert of Wurtemberg

Major Fairholme
In attendance on HRH The Prince
Rupert of Bavaria

Colonel J R Slade CB
In attendance on TRH The Prince and
Princess of Bulgaria

Colonel M Bell CB VC
In attendance on
The Chinese Special Ambassador

Colonel H D Browne
In attendance on HRH The Hereditary
Grand Duke of Luxembourg

Colonel D Dawson
In attendance on
The French Special Ambassador

Captain von Baumbach
In attendance on
HRH The Duke of Connaught KG

Colonel H Knollys RA In attendance on
Comptroller and Private secretary to
HRH The Princess Charles of Denmark

Colonel A Egerton CB In attendance on
Comptroller and Treasurer to HRH The
Duke of Connaught KG

Captain Hon H Napier
In attendance on
The Envoy of the Hawaiian Islands

Major Curtis P Iaukea
In attendance on
The Envoy of the Hawaiian Islands

Colonel Hon C Eliot Comptroller and
Treasurer to TRH The Prince and
Princess Christian of Schleswig-Holstein

Colonel S Waller
In attendance on
HIM The Empress Frederick

Lt Colonel C V Hume RA
In attendance on
HRH The Crown Prince of Siam

Colonel E H Sartorious VC
In attendance on
HRH The Crown Prince of Siam

Captain Sir M Fitzgerald, Bart, Knight
of Kerry Extra Equerry to HRH The
Duke of Connaught KG

Colonel H Parr CB CMG
In attendance on The Special
Ambassador of the United States

Colonel Needham
In attendance on TRH The Crown
Prince and Princess of Italy

Colonel Wardrop
In attendance on HI&RH The Archduke
Francis Ferdinand

Colonel C Larking
In attendance on
Prince Mohammed Ali Pasha of Egypt

The Earl of Denbigh
Lord in Waiting to the Queen
In attendance on HI&RH The Archduke
Francis Ferdinand

Colonel G Ponsonby In attendance on
Munir Pasha

Colonel J M Grierson In attendance on
HRH The Prince Albert of Prussia

Colonel Brabazon CB In attendance on
The French Special Ambassador

*Figure 39. Sergeant,
Queensland Mounted Rifles.*

*Figure 38. South Australian
Mounted Rifles.*

Colonel Pejanovitch
In attendance on
The Hereditary Prince of Montenegro

Colonel Djurcovitch
In attendance on
The Hereditary Prince of Montenegro

Major The Hon C Harbord, Groom in
Waiting to the Queen In attendance on
The Hereditary Prince of Montenegro

Colonel Clements
In attendance on
HIH The Grand Duke Cyril of Russia

Lt Colonel Murata
In attendance on
HIH The Prince Arisugawa of Japan

Captain Beaumont RN
In attendance on
HIH The Prince Arisugawa of Japan

Captain M P Maus
ADC to General Miles Commander-in-
Chief of the United States Army

Colonel Georgescu
ADC to HM The King of Roumania

Major C R Burn
In attendance on the deputation of The
Queen's Prussian Dragoons of the Guard

Baron de Grenadius Grancy, ADC to
HRH The Grand Duke of Hesse

Colonel Waters, In attendance on HIH
The Grand Duke Serge of Russia

Mr Min Young Chan
In attendance on
The Special Ambassador from Corea

Mr Min Shangbo
In attendance on
The Special Ambassador from Corea

Major A Cavendish
In attendance on
The Special Ambassador from Corea

Captain von Ruxleben
ADC to HRH The Hereditary Prince of
Saxe-Coburg and Gotha

Captain The Hon D J Monson
Comptroller and Equerry to HRH The
Duke of Saxe-Coburg and Gotha
(Duke of Edinburgh)

Count Zeppelin
ADC to HH The Prince Hermann of
Saxe-Weimar

Count Szapary
In attendance on
HRH The Prince Philip of Saxe-Coburg

Colonel Howard
In attendance on HRH The Prince
Frederick Augustus, Duke of Saxony

Baron von Oppell, In attendance on
HRH The Prince Frederick Augustus,
Duke of Saxony

Ist Lt von Metzsh, In attendance on
HRH The Prince Frederick Augustus,
Duke of Saxony

Count Reventlow Criminil, In attendance
on TRH The Grand Duke and Grand
Duchess of Mecklenburg-Strelitz

Lt General v Plessen, In attendance on
HRH The Prince Albert of Prussia
(Regent of Brunswick)

Major Freiherr v Stein, ADC to HRH
The Prince Albert of Prussia (Regent of
Brunswick)

Captain V Unger
ADC to HRH The Prince Albert of
Prussia (Regent of Brunswick)

Captain Enver Bey
In attendance on Munir Pacha

Brig General Nassir Pacha
In attendance on Munir Pacha

Major Surtees
In attendance on Munir Pacha

Captain Baron Cederstrom, ADC to
HRH Prince Eugene of Sweden

Captain Roeder, ADC to HRH Prince
Eugene of Sweden

Count G Gyldenstolpe, ADC to HRH
Prince Eugene of Sweden, First Equerry
to HM The King of Sweden

Figure 40. Queensland Mounted Rifles

Figure 41. Cape Mounted Rifles.

Lt Colonel Marcoff
ADC to HRH The Prince of Bulgaria

Major Petrew
ADC to HRH The Prince of Bulgaria

Captain Stoianow
ADC to HRH The Prince of Bulgaria

Lieutenant E v Le Bret-Nucourt
In attendance on
HRH The Prince Rupert of Bavaria

General Karim Khan
In attendance on
HIH The Prince Amir Khan of Persia

General Sir T Gordon KCIE CB
In attendance on
HIH The Prince Amir Khan of Persia

Lieutenant Count Maylath
In attendance on HI&RH The Archduke
Francis Ferdinand of Austria

Captain Baron de Bronn
In attendance on HI&RH The Archduke
Francis Ferdinand of Austria

Major v Winsloe
In attendance on
HSH The Prince of Schaumburg-Lippe

Colonel J Clerk CVO CSI
Extra Equerry to The Queen
Comptroller and Treasurer to
HRH The Princess Henry of Battenberg

Captain Othon V Stettin
In attendance on
HRH The Prince Rupert of Bavaria

Major General Sir C T Du Plat KCB
Extra Equerry to The Queen
In attendance on
HRH The Prince Albert of Prussia

Colonel A G Lucas, Suffolk Hussars
In attendance on
HRH The Duke of York KG

The Hon Derek Keppel
In attendance on
HRH The Duke of York KG

Major General Sir F de Winton GCMG
CB, Comptroller and Treasurer to HRH
The Duke of York KG

1st Lt Count v Degenfeld Schonburg
In attendance on
HRH The Duke Albert of Wurtemberg

Aziz Bey
In attendance on The Prince
Mohammed Ali Khan of Egypt

Said Zoulphicai Bey
In attendance on The Prince
Mohammed Ali Khan of Egypt

Lieutenant de Mellos, Personal ADC
to HRH The Duke of Oporto

Major d'Alburquerque, Personal ADC
to HRH The Duke of Oporto

Colonel Duval Telles
ADC to HM The King of Portugal

Senor Benites
In attendance on
The Spanish Special Ambassador

Colonel Humbert
ADC to The French Special Ambassador

Captain Reviers de Mauny
ADC to The French Special Ambassador

Captain Muller
In attendance on
HRH The Prince Henry of Prussia

Count Hahn
In attendance on
HRH The Prince Henry of Prussia

Admiral of the Fleet Sir J E Commerell
GCB VC, Groom in Waiting to The
Queen, In attendance on HRH The
Prince Henry of Prussia

Figure 42. Natal Carbineers.

Figure 43. Captain Ames, 2nd Life Guards, admiring the CMG worn by Lieutenant Colonel The Hon M Gifford, Rhodesia Horse. Colonel Gifford had lost his arm when wounded during the fighting in Mashonaland in 1896.

Lt General v Bilfinger, In attendance on
HRH The Duke Albert of Wurtemberg

Captain G L Holford
Equerry to HRH The Prince of Wales
In attendance on HRH The Prince
Eugene of Sweden and Norway

Captain Evers
In attendance on
HRH The Prince Waldemar of
Denmark

Major General A Ellis CSI
Equerry to HRH The Prince of Wales
In attendance on HRH The Prince
Waldemar of Denmark

Captain The Hon A Greville, Extra
Equerry to HRH The Prince of Wales
In attendance on The Duke of
Sotomayor, Special Ambassador of Spain

Colonel Sir Nigel Kingscote KCB
Extra Equerry to
HRH The Prince of Wales

Colonel Lord Wantage KCB VC
Extra Equerry to
The Prince of Wales

HE Herr v Schon
In attendance on
HRH The Duke of Saxe-Coburg
and Gotha

General Sir H Lynedoch Gardiner,
KCVO CB, Groom in Waiting and Extra
Equerry to The Queen, In attendance on
HRH The Prince Rupert of Bavaria

General Sir Dighton Probyn
GCVO KCB KCSI VC
Comptroller and Treasurer to HRH The
Prince of Wales

Lt General Terzaghi, First ADC
In attendance on
HRH The Crown Prince of Italy

Major Cavaliere Viganoni, ADC
In attendance on
HRH The Crown Prince of Italy

Captain Cavaliere Merli Miglietti, ADC
In attendance on
HRH The Crown Prince of Italy

HE Count Otto Traun
In attendance on HI&RH The Archduke
Francis Ferdinand of Austria

Baron Reischach
In attendance on
HIM The Empress Frederic

Baron v Roeder
In attendance on
HRH The Princess of Saxe-Meiningen

The Lord Harris GCSI GCIE, Lord in
Waiting to The Queen, In attendance on
HIM The Empress Frederic

The Earl of Kintore GCMG
Lord in Waiting to The Queen

The Earl of Gosford KP
Lord in Waiting to
HRH The Prince of Wales

The Earl of Clarendon
Lord in Waiting to The Queen
In attendance on TRH The Crown
Prince and Princess of Italy

Figure 44. Royal Malta Militia

Figure 45. Officers of Royal Malta Artillery

*Figure 46. Royal Canadian Artillery.
Non-commissioned Officers in working dress.*

(Foreign Naval and Military Attaches)

Major Shiba
Military Attache, Japan

Lieutenant Colwell, USN
Naval Attache, United States

Lt Colonel Count de Pontavice de
Heussey, Military Attache, France

Lt Colonel Don Jose Riberu Lopez
Military Attache, Spain

Major General HSH Prince Louis
Esterhazy
Military Attache, Austria-Hungary

Captain Gulich
Naval Attache, Germany

Colonel Yermoloff
Military Attache, Russia

Major General Nelson A Miles
Commander-in-Chief United States
Army

General Hagron, Chief of the Military
Household of the President of the
French Republic

(Officers of the 1st Prussian Dragoons of the Guard ("Queen of Great Britain and Ireland"))

2nd Lieutenant v Studnitz

1st Lieutenant v Gerlach

Lieutenant Baron v Moeller Lilienstern

Major v Arnim

Lt Colonel v Falkenhayn

(Deputation of Indian Officers, Imperial Service Troops)

Major F H R Drummond (see Note C)
11th Prince of Wales's Own Bengal Lancers

Risaldar Dhan Singh
Bhavnagar

Risaldar Major Kishan Singh,
Naba Lancers

Risaldar Major Didar Singh,
Jind Lancers

Risaldar Hara Singh,
Kapurthala Lancers

Commandant Daud Khan,
Ulwar

Risaldar Adbul Majid Khan,
Bahawalpur Lancers

Captain Mir Hashim Ali Khan,
Hyderabad

Commandant Nand Singh,
Patiala

Commandant Rai Bahadur Thakur Dip
Singh, Bikanir

Commandant Chartru Singh,
Bhurtpore

Risaldar Major Sunayat Singh,
Kashmir

Superintendent Rai Bahadur Dhunpat
Rai, Jaipur

Commandant Nazir Khan,
Rampur

Commandant Mirza Kurim Beg,
Bhopal

Commandant Govind Ras Matkar,
Indore

Commandant Abdul Ganny,
Gwalior

Captain F Angelo, 9th Bengal Lancers

Colonel H Melliss CSI, Inspector-
General of Imperial Service Troops in
India

(See note C)

Lieutenant Colonel Maharaj Dhiraj Sir
Pertab Singh KCSI, ADC to HRH The
Prince of Wales, Regent of Jodhpur

(Envoys) (See note D)

Figure 47. Colonel Maharajah Sir Pertab Singh KCSI, Jodhpur Lancers.

(The Carriage Procession)

Fifteen Carriages bearing visiting representatives of foreign countries and members of the Royal Family, in ascending order of precedence.

Sixteenth Carriage (four black horses) conveying:

HRH The Duke of Saxe-Coburg and Gotha KG
HRH The Princess Louise of Great Britain and Ireland (Marchioness of Lorne)
HRH The Princess of NAples
HIH The Empress Frederic of Germany

The following Equerries rode by this Carriage:

Colonel The Hon Henry Byng CB
Lieutenant F E G Ponsonby

(Colonial Escort) (See note E)

(First Part of Sovereign's Escort)

First Part of Escort of 2nd Life Guards

Major The Hon H C Legge MVO, Equerry to The Queen

(Royal Princes and Representatives)

The Baron Pawel V Rammingen KCB	HSH The Prince Alexander of Teck	The Duke of Fife KT	The Marquis of Lorne KT
HSH The Prince Francis of Teck	HSH The Prince Adolphus of Teck		HH The Prince Albert of Schleswig-Holstein
HIH The Prince Amir Khan of Persia	The Prince Mohammed Ali Pacha of Egypt		The Prince Mahit of Siam
HH The Duke of Teck GCB	HH The Prince Christian Victor of Schleswig-Holstein GCB		HSH The Prince Louis of Battenberg GCB
HRH The Prince of Bulgaria	HRH The Prince Philip of Saxe-Coburg GCB		HH The Prince Danilo (Crown Prince of Montenegro)
HH The Prince Aribert of Anhalt GCB	HH The Prince Hermann of Saxe-Weimar		HSH The Prince Adolph of Schaumburg-Lippe GCB

Figure 48. Artillery and Infantry Volunteers of Western Australia.

HIH The Grand Duke Cyril
of Russia

HRH The Prince Charles
of Denmark GCB

HH The Prince Frederic Charles
of Hesse

HIH The Prince Arisugawa
of Japan

HRH The Hereditary Prince
of Saxe-Coburg and Gotha

HRH The Hereditary Grand Duke
of Luxemburg

HRH The Duke
of Oporto

HRH The Prince Eugene
of Sweden and Norway

HRH The Duke Albert
of Wurtemberg

HRH The Prince Rupert
of Bavaria

HRH The Prince Christian
of Schleswig-Holstein KG

HRH The Prince Frederick Augustus,
Duke of Saxony

HRH The Duke
of York KG

HRH The Crown Prince
of Siam

HRH The Prince Waldemar
of Denmark

HRH The Prince Henry
of Prussia KG

HRH The Prince Albert
of Prussia (Prince Regent of Brunswick)

HIH The Grand Duke Serge
of Russia GCB

HRH The Prince
of Naples KG

HI&RH The Archduke Francis
Ferdinand of Austria-Hungary

HRH The Grand Duke
of Hesse GCB

(Escort of Indian Cavalry)

Lt Colonel J C F Gordon, 6th Prince of Wales's Bengal Cavalry

Major A Phayre 3rd Queen's Own Bombay Cavalry

Captain C F Campbell 6th Prince of Wales's Bengal Cavalry

Rissaldar Major Izzat Khan
17th Bengal Cavalry

Rissaldar Major Khan
Bahadur Khan, 10th Bengal
Lancers

Rissaldar Major Baha-ud-din
Khan Central India Horse,
ADC to HE The Viceroy

Rissaldar Major Abdul Aziz
5th Bengal Cavalry

Rissaldar Major Hussain
Khan, 2nd Lancers
Hyderabad Contingent

Rissaldar Major Kesur Singh
5th Punjab Cavalry

Rissaldar Major Sher Singh
13th Bengal Lancers

Rissaldar Major Hukam
Singh 16th Bengal Cavalry

Rissaldar Major Ali
Mohammed Khan,
2nd Bengal Cavalry

Rissaldar Major Faiz Khan
6th Bombay Cavalry

Rissaldar Major Mohammed
Umar Khan,
5th Bombay Cavalry

Rissaldar Major Mangul
Singh, 3rd Bengal Cavalry

Rissaldar Nadir Khan,
9th Bengal Lancers

Rissaldar Jehangir Khan,
1st Bombay Lancers

Rissaldar Kaddam Khan 4th
Bengal Cavalry

Rissaldar Major Mehrab Ali
Khan, 3rd Lancers Hyderabad
Contingent

Figure 49. Chinese Submarine Miners of Hong Kong Engineers.

Figure 50. Malay States Guides.

Figure 51. New South Wales Artillery.

43

Rissaldar Gurdat Singh, 12th Bengal Cavalry	Rissaldar Net Ram, 7th Bengal Cavalry	Rissaldar Makbul Khan, 8th Bengal Cavalry	Rissaldar Mir Haidar Shah 7th Bombay Lancers

Jemadar Abdul Karim Khan
Viceroy's Bodyguard

Subadar Mohammed Bey, 1st
Madras Lancers

Major J G Turner Viceroy's Bodyguard attached to Maharaj Dhiraj Sir Pertab Singh

Field Marshal Viscount Wolseley KP GCB GCMG, Commander-in-Chief

Seventeenth Carriage (eight cream horses)

HRH The Princess Helena of Great Britain and Ireland (Princess Christian of Schleswig-Holstein)

HRH The Princess of Wales

The Queen

The following rode by this carriage:

Field Marshal HRH The Duke of Cambridge KG

Field Marshal HRH The Prince of Wales KG

General HRH The Duke of Connaught and Strathearn KG

(Mounted Military Suite)

Captain of Escort, Major S Cuninghame 2nd Life Guards	The Standard (Sovereign's Standard of 2nd Life Guards)	Field Officer of Escort, Colonel The Earl of Dundonald CB 2nd Life Guards	Chief of Staff, Major General Lord Methuen CB CMG
The Earl of Coventry, Master of the Buckhounds	The Marquis of Lothian KT, Gold Stick of Scotland	General Earl Howe GCB, Gold Stick in Waiting	The Duke of Portland GCVO, Master of the Horse

Lieutenant Colonel Sir A J Bigge KCB CMG, Private Secretary
and Equerry to The Queen

Lieutenant Colonel The Right Hon Sir F I Edwards KCB
Keeper of the Privy Purse and Extra Equerry to The Queen

Figure 52. Drum Major Goodman, London Scottish Rifle Volunteers.

Figure 53. Sergeant W J Gordon VC and another soldier, West India Regiment.

Figure 54. West India Regiment.

Major General Sir J C McNeill KCB KCMG VC, Equerry in Waiting

Lieutenant Colonel A Davidson MVO, Equerry in Waiting

Major General Sir H P Ewart KCB, Crown Equerry

Colonel L J Oliphant Grenadier Guards, Field Officer in Brigade Waiting

Major General S Clarke CMG, Equerry to HRH The Prince of Wales

Lieutenant Colonel Sir S M Lockhart Bart, 1st Life Guards, Silver Stick in Waiting

Lieutenant Colonel A C Fitz George CB, Equerry to HRH The Duke of Cambridge

Captain The Hon W Bagot Grenadier Guards, Adjutant in Brigade Waiting

Captain B Cook 1st Life Guards, Silver Stick Adjutant in Waiting

Six Royal Grooms

Rear Part of Escort, 2nd Life Guards

Mounted Detachment, Royal Irish Constabulary

Squadron, Royal Horse Guards

Notes:

A. Canadian Militia Cavalry were represented by small detachments of The Governor General's Bodyguard, 1st Hussars, 3rd Dragoons, 5th Princess Louise's Dragoon Guards, 8th Princess Louise's New Brunswick Hussars, 10th Queen's Own Canadian Hussars, 12th Manitoba Dragoons, and the King's Canadian Hussars (See Fig 32).

B. Canadian Militia Infantry were represented by small detachments of seventeen Regiments including The Governor General's Foot Guards, 2nd Queen's Own Rifles, 3rd Victoria Rifles, 5th Royal Scots, 10th Royal Grenadiers, 48th Highlanders and 62nd Fusiliers. (See appendix 4)

C. Accompanying the "Deputation of Indian Officers of Imperial Service Troops" (that is those furnished by the rulers of Indian States) on the procession were two officers apparently in the uniform of the 11th Bengal Lancers. One was Major Drummond. The name of the other has not yielded to the author's research.

D. Two envoys rode in the Procession, those of the Hawaiian Islands and of Corea.

E. The Colonial Escort, under the command of Colonel Lasseter of the New South Wales forces, consisted of: nine Canadian cavalrymen, nine New South Wales cavalrymen, three men of the South Australian Mounted Rifles, two of the Queensland Mounted Rifles, four of the New Zealand Mounted Rifles, two of the Cape Mounted Rifles, two Natal Carbineers, two Trinidad cavalrymen and one man of the Ceylon Mounted Rifles.

F. Despite research, it has not been possible to determine finally the order in which all troops marched in the Procession. The list above has been based on the rather sketchy information in the London Gazette modified by additional evidence such as photographs. Any further information on this or any related matter will be gratefully received by the author and will be submitted to the Editor of one or other of the Victorian Military Society publications.

Figure 55. Hong Kong Regiment.

Appendix 2
Notes on the Colonial Contingents

These notes are intended to give some social information about each of the smaller Colonial elements of the Procession including a brief description of the uniforms worn. Where the information given here conflicts with that shown in the centrefold by Frank Dadd, the former should be regarded as correct for 22nd June 1897 in London. In such cases, for example the North West Mounted Police, the artist has shown the service dress worn at home rather than the full dress, review order, worn (where it was provided) in London.

Many of the Colonial corps are described as wearing khaki or khaki drab. This covers a wide range of shades from a brownish type of khaki to the colour of khaki drill or "stone". Some further research is recommended before making deductions in this area.

Although limitations of space have precluded full descriptions and illustrations of the British military units, it was felt that they could not simply be omitted. The notes below therefore include some brief remarks concerning certain individuals and Regiments chiefly to guide the reader to other, fuller, sources of information.

THE COLONIAL PROCESSION

1. *Royal Horse Guards.* Four soldiers of the Royal Horse Guards led the Colonial Procession in mounted review order. Their uniform of blue tunic with scarlet facings, steel helmet, steel cuirasse, white buckskin breeches with tall black boots was

Figure 56. 5th Royal Scots of Canada.

Figure 57. 3rd Victoria Rifles, Canada

Figure 58. Chinese members of Hong Kong Police.

Figure 59. Sierra Leone Frontier Force.

unchanged from 1890 and details can be found in Simkin's Soldiers Vol I (see Bibliography Item 16).

2. Field Marshal Lord Roberts. Born in 1832, Lord Roberts was commissioned from Addiscombe into the Bengal Artillery in 1851. He won his VC in the Indian Mutiny and spent much of his subsequent service in India culminating in the appointment there of Commander-in-Chief 1885-93. In 1895 he became Commander of the Forces in Ireland and came over from Dublin to head the Colonial Contingent on the Diamond Jubilee Procession. He was dressed as a Field Marshal in cocked hat with white over scarlet feathers; scarlet tunic with blue facings and gold embroidery on collar, cuffs and skirts, white buckskin breeches and tall black boots. His charger, a grey called Vonolel, had been with him for years. It bore him on the famous march in 1880 from Kabul to Kandahar (the title he took for his peerage) and wore on its breastplate the medals for that campaign. (See Figs 15 and 29)

3. Canadian Contingent – Cavalry Element. See Appendix 4.

4. North West Mounted Police. See Appendix 4.

5. New South Wales Lancers. See Appendix 3.

6. New South Wales Mounted Rifles. See Appendix 3.

7. Victoria Mounted Rifles. See Appendix 3.

8. New Zealand Mounted Rifles. Khaki slouch hat with plaited pagri, though much slimmer than that affected by the Victoria Mounted Rifles; brim turned up at the right and secured with a red cord to a button. Khaki drab jacket with breast pockets, scarlet collar and pointed cuffs, metal collar badges. Matching breeches with scarlet stripe. Brown leather waistbelt with snake clasp. Black leather boots. Officers had gold braid edgings to collar and cuffs and wore a brown leather sam browne belt.

9. South Australian Mounted Rifles. See Appendix 3.

10. Queensland Mounted Rifles. See Appendix 3.

11. Cape Mounted Rifles. The Jubilee Detachment consisted of Lt W H B Phillips and 15 other ranks. The uniform was a white helmet without badge but with dome and spike, and curbchain, of black metal; jacket of rifle green edged all round with black braid, fastened by hook and eye without buttons; rifle green breeches with black stripe; black boots; brown leather bandolier over the left shoulder, and brown leather pistol case and ammunition pouch both on a rarrow brown leather strap over the right shoulder; sword belt worn under the jacket with black slings. The officer's jacket was braided as for Rifles without facings; the black patent leather pouch belt had white metal fittings of boss, whistle and chain with a large regimental badge between. (see fig 41)

12. Natal Carbineers. Khaki slouch hat turned up at the left with a badge; leather chinstrap. Khaki drab jacket with breast pockets; no facings. Breeches to match. Brown leather boots, belt, gauntlets and bandolier – the latter distinctive because it was worn, unusually, over the right shoulder.. (see fig 42)

13. Ceylon Mounted Infantry. White helmet with white pagri, white metal regimental badge, white metal curbchain, dome and spike. Scarlet tunic with white metal buttons; blue collar edged all round with white piping; blue pointed cuffs edged and surmounted with austrian knot, all in white cord or tubular braid. Khaki drab breeches with brown boots; brown leather

belt and bandolier over the left shoulder.

14. Trinidad Yeomanry. Captain E W Lack and 8 men. Khaki slouch hat with brown leather band round base of crown; brim turned up at the left and secured with white metal badge on a green cloth ground. Khaki drab jacket with breast pockets; cavalry pattern white metal shoulder chains. Matching breeches. Brown boots with light khaki canvas gaiters secured with four brown leather straps. Brown leather bandolier over left shoulder. Sword belt under jacket with white leather slings. Officer has dark green feathered plume on left side of hat and brown leather sam browne belt.

15. Cyprus Military Police. Major A E Kershaw, two Cypriot officers and 15 other ranks. Uniform: Red fez with black tassel. Plain dark blue sleeved zouave jacket edged with red braid worn over dark blue waistcoat which fastened with five small yellow metal buttons down the front. Red cummerbund. Dark blue breeches and black knee boot. Brown leather belt with pistol case and ammunition pouch. Unlike all the other Colonial corps, this unit brought its own saddles and saddlecloths to Britain: the saddle is of an oriental type with very wide flaps; the saddle cloth was small with rounded corners, dark blue in colour with an edging design of two lines of red braid with a zigzag design between; in the rear corners, the letters CMP. The horse furniture was not of British Army pattern but was probably of brown leather; the bridle, martingale and even the crupper were decorated with large red tassels.

16. Rhodesian Horse. Captain The Hon M Gifford (who had lost his right arm during active service in Matabeleland in 1896 – see Fig 43) and 10 other ranks.Khaki slouch hat with khaki pagri; brim turned up at the left. Khaki drab jacket with breast pockets. Khaki breeches and puttees. Brown leather waistbelt and brace as for sam browne but with loops for pistol rounds; brown leather bandolier over left shoulder.

17. Band of 1st Middlesex Rifle Volunteers. Helmet, tunic and trousers of rifle green with black leather equipment.

18. Royal Malta Regiment of Militia. (See Figs 44) White helmet with yellow metal curbchain, dome and spike. Scarlet tunic with dark blue facings as for Royal Regiment; white metal collar badges. Blue trousers with scarlet welt. White waistbelt. Black boots.

19. Royal Malta Artillery. White helmet with yellow metal curbchain, dome and ball ornament. Dark blue tunic and trousers as for Royal Field Artillery: scarlet collar; scarlet piping on the front and skirts; yellow cord edging to collar and cuffs, and forming austrian knot above the cuffs. Officers as for Royal Artillery except for the special patterns of helmet plate and sabretache (see Fig 45).

20. Royal Canadian Artillery. See Appendix 4.

21. Trinidad Field Artillery Volunteers. White helmet with white metal curbchain, dome and ball ornament; large white metal grenade badge. Dark blue tunic and trousers as for Royal Artillery: scarlet collar and piping to front and skirts; white cord edging to collar and cuffs, and forming austrian knot above cuffs; white metal grenade collar badges. White buff belt with white metal clasp.

Figure 62. Sentry, Gold Coast Hausas. Note that in Africa these troops worked in bare feet. Wearing unaccustomed boots in London gave them very sore feet!

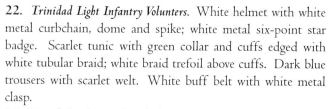

Figure 60. Sergeants of Gold Coast Hausas.

Figure 61. Captain D Houston, Gold Coast Hausas.

22. Trinidad Light Infantry Volunteers. White helmet with white metal curbchain, dome and spike; white metal six-point star badge. Scarlet tunic with green collar and cuffs edged with white tubular braid; white braid trefoil above cuffs. Dark blue trousers with scarlet welt. White buff belt with white metal clasp.

23. Trinidad Police. White helmet with white metal curbchain, dome and spike; white metal badge. Dark blue jacket and trousers, without facings, without piping; white metal buttons, shoulder title and whistle chain. White waistbelt and pouch.

24. Jamaica Artillery, Bermuda Artillery and St Lucia Artillery. All these seem to have worn essentially the same uniform. This was: white helmet, probably with white pagri and yellow metal curbchain, dome and ball ornament. Blue Royal Artillery frock, that is a plain 5 button jacket without piping down the front nor on the skirts; scarlet collar with yellow metal grenade badges, edged along the bottom with yellow braid; self-material cuffs edged with yellow cord to form a trefoil above; blue shoulder straps edged with yellow cord; yellow metal buttons. Blue trousers with RA pattern broad scarlet stripe. Black boots. White buff waistbelt.

25. Jamaica Militia Infantry. White helmet; yellow metal badge to front; yellow metal curbchain, dome and spike. Scarlet tunic piped white down the front and on the skirts; dark blue collar and cuffs; the collar edged all round with white tubular braid; the cuffs edged with white tubular braid forming an austrian knot above; yellow metal buttons. Dark blue trousers with scarlet welt. Black boots. White buff waistbelt.

26. Perth Artillery Volunteers. See Appendix 3.

27. Western Australia Infantry Volunteers. See Appendix 3.

28. Hong Kong Engineers. Three "Eastern Submarine Mining" Companies of Royal Engineers existed. It seems that the Hong Kong Company had British officers and chinese other ranks, possibly Indians as well. A detachment of the Chinese attended the Jubilee celebrations and their dress was among the more unusual to be seen (see Fig 24). While they seem to have worn a Chinese type of headdress in Britain, possibly coloured blue with a brass ball ornament on top, their dress at home seems to have been the more conventional lightweight sunhat – see Fig 49. The rest of the ensemble was as shown: a long khaki drill jacket fastened with ties in the Chinese style, khaki drill trousers and some form of white cotton stocking or hosetop (the contemporary magazine Navy & Army Illustrated thought that they covered puttees but this seems unlikely). Black shoes. White buff belt with yellow metal clasp. Note that these men all had very long plaited pigtails.

29. Malay States Guides. The Regiment was raised in 1896 and was composed of Indian soldiers with British officers. Dress: Pagri of green and yellow tied according to race and religion. Tunic scarlet with dark green collar and cuffs; the tunic piped white down the front and on the skirts; the collar edged all round with white braid; the scarlet shoulder straps edged with white braid; the cuffs edged with white braid which formed a trefoil above. Dark blue trousers with black boots and white knee length gaiters. White buff waistbelt with yellow metal clasp. (See Fig 50)

30. Malay Police. This force consisted of Indian and Malay policemen commanded by senior British officers. The working daytime uniform for all was khaki drill with different headdress by race. British officers had in addition a white tunic and trousers with brown or black leather accoutrements for full dress. For duty at night, a blue serge uniform was provided and it seems that it was in this dress that men paraded for the Jubilee. For a Malay policeman, the dress was: field service cap of dark blue with two buttons at the front and a crown badge. Dark blue frock and trousers without facings or embellishments of any kind except for a number on the shoulder straps. Black boots and white calf-length gaiters. Black leather belt with white metal clasp.

31. *Singapore Engineers.* (See serial 28 above: this was another of the Eastern Companies. Dress for Malay soldiers (see Fig 24): Dark blue pillbox cap with yellow band. Khaki drill 5 button tunic with breast pockets. Khaki drill trousers. Black boots. White buff waistbelt with yellow metal clasp.

32. *West Indies Royal Engineers.* White helmet; yellow metal badge in front; yellow metal curbchain, dome and spike. Scarlet Royal Engineers pattern frock, that is a plain 5 button scarlet jacket without piping on front or skirts; dark blue collar edged all round with yellow cord; dark blue cuffs coming to a shallow point edged with yellow cord which forms a single loop above; shoulder straps in the form of a loop of yellow cord; yellow metal buttons. Dark blue trousers with scarlet stripe. Black boots. White buff waistbelt.

33. *Mauritius Royal Engineers.* White helmet; yellow metal curbchain, dome and spike. Remainder as for serial 32 above.

34. *Malta Militia Submarine Miners.* This detachment paraded in an unusual but workmanlike uniform, much like that of serial 32 above. The headdress was a naval rating's cap with a white cover and a "tally" proclaiming "Submarine Miners". The jacket was a plain dark blue 5 button frock with no breast pockets and trousers to match. Black boots. White buff waistbelt with a gilt clasp. (See Fig 24)

35. *Hong Kong Garrison Artillery.* There were four Companies of Royal Garrison Artillery located in Hong Kong with Indian soldiers. Dress: scarlet pagri ending for some races (see Fig 24) with a yellow fringe falling to one side, or possibly to the front. Remainder of uniform as for West Indies Artillery (at serial 24 above except that the Hong Kong unit wore long dark blue puttees).

36. *Mauritius Royal Artillery.* There were two Companies of Garrison Artillery on Mauritius manned, as in Hong Kong, with Indian soldiers under British senior officers. Dress (see Fig 24): yellow and blue pagri. Remainder of uniform as for West Indies Artillery (serial 24 above).

37. *Ceylon Royal Engineers.* Khaki drill or pale drab pagri with red fringe falling forward from centre. Remainder as for West Indies Royal Engineers (serial 32 above).

38. *New South Wales Artillery.* See Appendix 3.

39. *New South Wales Enginers.* See Appendix 3.

40. *London Scottish Rifle Volunteers.* All ranks of the London Scottish, including the pipers wore doublet and kilt of hodden grey (which has a pink tinge). See Fig 52 which shows the redoubtable and well known figure of Drum Major Goodman. His dress: Dark blue glengarry with blue toorie; black binding

Figure 63. Royal Niger Hausas.

and tails; white metal thistle badge with black feathers behind; royal blue collar and gauntlet cuffs; blue edging down the chest and blue braid in the form of long buttonholes in threes on each inverness flap; collar eddged with silver braid; cuffs and inverness flaps edged with 1/2 inch silver lace; false buton holes in threes on the cuffs of silver russia braid; butons and collar badges of white metal; shoulder straps of twisted silver cord. Waistbelt and sporran cantle of brown leather, the former with white metal clasp and the latter with white metal thistle badge (as on the glengarry); sporran hair of a greyish brown colour; tassels black from white metal holders. Plaid of hodden grey with white metal brooch. Drum Major's belt of royal blue with silver embroidery and edging of 1 inch silver lace. Diced hosetops of blue-grey, royal blue and yellow; white spats with white buttons; black boots. Staff black with silver embellishments.

41. *West India Regiment.* The Regiment, then of three battalions, was represented by one officer and 16 other ranks of the 2nd Battalion (see Fig 54) one of whom was Sergeant W J Gordon who had won the VC in West Africa in 1892. The Officer was dressed as regular British infantry of the day stationed in a colony: white helmet with white pagri; gilt curbchain, dome and spike. Scarlet tunic with white collar and pointed cuffs; the collar edged on top and front with 5/8 inch gold lace and along the bottom with gold russia; the cuffs edged with 5/8 inch gold lace, traced inside and out with gold russia forming a crow's foot below and a small austrian knot above; white piping down the front and in two vertical lines on

Figure 64. Captain O Ames, 2nd Life Guards.

thre rear skirts falling from two buttons at the waist; eight gilt buttons down the chest; twisted gold cords on the shoulders. Dark blue trousers with scarlet welt. Black boots. Crimson sash over the left shoulder. White buff waistbelt with gilt clasp; white buff sword slings. Nickel plated sword hilt and scabbard; gold and crimson sword knot and acorn. Dress of other ranks (see Fig 53): round red cap with white tassel; white twisted turban around the cap. White sleeved waistcoat (or shell jacket) with a low collar edged yellow all round and fastened with some 20 small yellow metal buttons; self-material pointed cuffs were edged with yellow braid; over the white jacket, a scarlet sleeveless waistcoat edged all round with yellow braid and having a design of zigzags in narrow yellow braid down the chest. Dark blue baggy trousers with yellow piping down the front and side seams. White stockings with short white gaiters over black boots. White buff waistbelt with gilt clasp.

42. Hong Kong Regiment. This Regiment was raised in India in 1892 for service in Hong Kong and disbanded in 1902. The dress of Indian other ranks was (see Figs 26 and 55): blue pagri with prominent transverse stripes of red and yellow showing at the front; Fig 26 shows an interesting variety of pagris by tribal background. Scarlet kurta with very low collar; the front opening edged with yellow piping; scarlet pointed cuffs edged with narrow yellow braid forming a trefoil above; breast pockets with the flaps edged with yellow piping; scarlet shoulder straps with yellow metal titles; yellow metal buttons. Dark blue full trousers (known as knickerbockers) with scarlet welts; dark blue puttees in service dress but white gaiters (in London and) in review order. Black boots. (Probably) brown leather waistbelt with yellow metal clasp. Note that the rather

plump Indian officer with the badge in his pagri on the right of the group in Fig 26 belongs to the Regiment: his dress corresponded in colours to the above.

43. Canadian Infantry. See Appendix 4.

44. British Guiana Constulary. The police force of this colony was armed and semi-military. Dress (see Fig 23): Flat white cap with plain black peak and white neck curtain. Dark blue 5 button frock and trousers without any embellishment except a whistle chain between top and second buttonholes; white metal buttons. Brown leather waistbelt with white metal clasp.

45. Ceylon Garrison Artillery. This unit, a single Company, was composed of volunteers and their uniform, aside from headdress, matched that of many RA Volunteer units at Home: White helmet with white pagri; white metal curbchain, dome and ball ornament. Dark blue frock and trousers as for West Indies Artillery (serial 24 above) except that the narrow braid on the collar and cuffs was white instead of yellow; white metal gernade collar badges; white metal buttons.

46. Ceylon Light Infantry Volunteers. (See Fig 25) White helmet with white pagri; white metal curbchain, dome and spike. Scarlet tunic with dark blue collar and shallow-pointed cuffs; the collar piped white along the bottom only; white metal collar badges; cuffs edged with narrow white braid which formed an austrian knot above; front of tunic edged white; seven white metal buttons; two vertical lines of white piping on rear skirts falling from two butons at the waist. Dark blue trousers with scarlet welt and long white gaiters. Black boots. White buff waistbelt with white metal clasp.

47. British North Borneo Police. This force was part military and composed of several races including Dyaks. Their dress was: scarlet pillbox cap with yellow metal lion badge. Khaki drill jacket and trousers with khaki puttees and black boots. Waistbelt of brown leather with yellow metal clasp.

48. Hong Kong Police. The force consisted of European, Indian and Chinese other ranks under British officers. It was semi-military and the British and Indian other ranks were armed with carbines; the Chinese other ranks had bayonets only. Dress was as follows: *Europeans and Indians:* Dark blue tunic without facings; collar piped white all round and bearing in white metal the man's number; white edging down the front of the tunic which fastened with eight white metal buttons; shoulder straps of twisted white cord. Dark blue trousers with white welt. Black boots. Brown leather waistbelt. For Europeans, a white helmet with blue pagri and white metal curbchain, dome and spike. For Indians, a scarlet pagri. *Chinese:* See Fig 58, chinese lightweight sun hat, shown here with a crown marked on it possibly in blue (but note from Fig 27 that this crown cannot be seen on the hats worn in England). Shapeless blue blouse fastened with five white metal buttons; low blue collar piped white along the bottom and bearing the man's number in white metal. Brown leather waistbelt with white metal clasp. Dark blue trousers; white cotton gaiters or hosetops probably similar to those worn by Hong Kong Engineers (Serial 28 above) and local pattern shoes – though it may well have been that they wore black shoes or boots in London. All these policemen, of all races, wore a whistle chain

Figure 65. Captain, Royal Navy. *Figure 66. Midshipman (left) and Cadets (right), Royal Navy.* *Figure 67. Petty Officer Seamen, Royal Navy.*

in the area of the second and third buttonholes.

49. *London Irish Rifle Volunteers.* Rifle green helmet, tunic and trousers with black equipment.

50. *Gold Coast Hausa Constabulary.* This unit was semi-military and in fact was re-titled the Gold Coast Regiment of the West African Frontier Force in 1901. The detachment which travelled to England for the Diamond Jubilee consisted of Captain Davidson-Houston, an african officer and 22 other ranks. The officers' dress was an elaborate zouave style of dark blue with black frogging loops (see Fig 61). The other ranks (see Fig 60) wore a red cap with a red tassel; a plain dark blue sleeved waistcoat or shell jacket fastened down the front (invisibly) with hooks and eyes; over this, a dark blue sleeveless waistcoat which was edged all round, including around the armholes, with red braid; there was a black leather patch on the left shoulder to protect the garment from the rifle when this was carried at the slope. Red cummerbund and black leather weaistbelt with yellow metal snake clasp. Full dark blue trousers with scarlet welt. Dark blue stockings or hosetops and black boots; short white gaiters.

51. *Royal Niger Company Hausa Constabulary.* This was the police force of the Royal Niger Company whose territories were taken over by the Crown from 1st January 1900. The detachment was of 2 officers and 15 other ranks. Their dress (see Fig 63) was a workmanlike khaki drill jacket and knickerbockers. The jacket had no outside pockets nor embellishments except for five yellow metal buttons. Round red cap. Dark blue stockings and, in review order, black boots with short white gaiters. (Service dress seems to have been brown shoes without gaiters.) Brown leather waistbelt and equipment; yellow metal snake clasp.

52. *Sierra Leone Frontier Police.* The detachment consisted of Captain Blakeney and 15 other ranks. The officer's dress appears to be: white helmet with white pagri; white metal curbchain. dome and spike. Dark blue tunic braided as for Rifle Regiments. Black patent leather pouch-belt with silver or white metal fittings. Dark blue trousers with black boots. For other ranks: round red cap with blue tassel. Dark blue shirt/tunic tucked into the trousers; aside from badges of rank, appointment and proficiency, no embellishments except for three yellow metal buttons on the chest and two smaller ones on the breast pockets. Dark blue loose trousers gathered into dark blue puttees. Black boots. Red cummerbund and black leather waistbelt with yellow metal snake clasp.

53. *Lagos Constabulary.* It appears that the dress of this detachment was the same as that of the Gold Coast Constabulary (serial 50 above) except only that the Lagos Constabulary wore dark blue puttees without gaiters.

54. *Captain O Ames, 2nd Life Guards.* See Figs 43 and 64. The Press turned Captain Ames into something of a celebrity as the tallest man in the Army. Perhaps that had something to do with the command of the Prince of Wales that he should head the Queen's Procession. His uniform was much as that of the Life Guards today and consisted of: Nickel plate helmet with gilt badge and embellishments, and white plume. Scarlet tunic with dark blue collar and cuffs; gold embroidery on the collar, cuffs and rear skirts; gold shoulder cords and aiguillette; nickel plate cuirasse with gilt scales. Gold lace pouchbelt with blue flask cord. White buckskin breeches and tall black boots. Horse furniture of Regimental pattern with shabraque of dark blue cloth with broad band of gold lace edged with scarlet cloth all round; embroidered devices in gold and silver (Garter star). (For more detail of the uniform which was the same (except for the flask cord and small details such as the buttons) as the 1st Life Guards, see Bibliography item 16.)

55. *Four Troopers, 2nd Life Guards.* Their dress was exactly as for 1st Life Guards except: blue flask cord instead of red; white sheepskin over the saddle instead of black. (See Bibliography item 16)

56. *Royal Navy.* See Figs 65-67. Commissioned officers wore tailcoats with cocked hats, midshipmen wore shell jackets with waistcoat, collar and tie, and forage caps, warrant officers wore jackets with collar and tie, and forage caps, and ratings wore jumpers with wideawake straw hats. (Fig 68 was not taken on this occasion but in 1900 at Windsor of the parade of the landing party of HMS Powerful on their return from South Africa. It shows a 12 pdr gun and limber of the same type as those of the Royal Navy contingent on the Jubilee Procession.)

57. *Royal Artillery Mounted Band.* See Fig 69 for the drummer of this band. His uniform was a black busby with a scarlet bag and plume worn on the left; dark blue tunic embellished with gold braid; dark blue breeches with broad red stripe; dark blue shabraque and drum banners braided and embroidered in gold, silver and colours. Musicians wore the same uniform.

58. *Royal Horse Artillery.* All wore the same uniform: a black busby with scarlet bag, white plume and yellow lines; dark blue shell jacket with yellow cord loops across the chest, yellow cord embellishments on the back and on the dark blue cuffs; scarlet collar; dark blue breeches with broad red stripe. Sergeants and above had gold cord on their jackets. Fig 72 shows a gun and its gunners, technically a sub-division, of T Battery Royal Horse Artillery which rode in the Procession after the 10th and 15th Hussars.

59. *Cavalry.* As a representative example of the fifteen cavalry Regiments represented in the Procession, see at Fig 71 a photograph of the mounted band of the 6th Inniskilling Dragoons. The musicians' uniform was a white metal helmet with yellow metal fittings and a red plume; scarlet tunic with yellow collar, cuffs and shoulder straps all edged with yellow cord; dar blue breeches with a broad yellow stripe. The drummer's shabraque was dark blue with gold braid edging and embroidery in gold, silver and colours; the drum banners were yellow with gold braid edging and gold fringe, and embroidery in gold, silver (the Castle device) and colours.

60. *Field Marshal Lord Wolseley.* Born like his contemporary Frederick Roberts in Ireland, Wolseley received his first commission in 1852 in the 80th Foot (later the 2nd Bn South Staffordshire Regiment). Forty-three years later he was selected to be Commander-in-Chief in succession to HRH The Duke of Cambridge who had held that office for 40 years. During that time, Wolseley had fought his way, literally, up the ladder. He saw active service first in Burma, then with the 90th Light Infantry in the Crimea where he was badly wounded; from there to India for the Mutiny, and thus to China. By 1860, at the age of 27 years, he was a Lieutenant Colonel. There followed nine years on the staff in Canada culminating in command of troops engaged in the Red River Expedition. This was crowned with success for which he was rewarded with a KCMG. After that he was employed either in achieving reform of Army administration or in command of operations – Ashanti 1873-74, Zululand 1879-80, Egypt 1882-84. He was indeed the "very model of a modern Major General" as Gilbert and Sullivan felt obliged to point out. Undoubtedly, he was the best person to succeed Cambridge and though over 60 and threatened with reforms of his office with which he did not agree, he as ever did his best. On the day of the Jubilee Procession, he rode just ahead of the Queen herself feeling unwell due partly to the collected effects of many wounds over the years and partly to overwork and sheer exhaustion. As soon as the Jubilee was over he went into hospital for an operation on the glands of his neck. He soon recovered from the local effects of this but did not seem to regain completely his full vitality. In November 1900 he retired upon handing over the role of Commander-in-Chief to Lord Roberts who had just returned from the successful completion of the first stage of the Anglo-Boer War. Lord Wolseley died in March 1913, a year and a half before Lord Roberts – the former peacefully at home and the latter within earshot of the guns while on a visit to the troops in France.

Figure 68. 12 pdr gun and limber of Royal Navy (together weighing some 15 cwt).

Figure 69. Drummer, Royal Artillery Mounted Band.

Figure 71. Mounted Band, 6th Inniskilling Dragoons.

Figure 70. Field Marshal Viscount Wolseley, Commander-in-Chief 1895-1900.

Figure 72. 12 Pdr Gun and Gunners of T Battery, Royal Horse Artillery.

53

Appendix 3
Notes on the Australian Contingents

THE AUSTRALIAN FORCES

1. *General Background.* In 1897, the Australian States were still autonomous. The Commonwealth was not enacted until July 1900 and did not take effect, so far as military forces were concerned, until March 1901. When therefore the Government in London decided to ask colonial representatives to the Diamond Jubilee celebrations, the invitations were sent directly to the six States. In every case, the State Premier travelled to London and all States except Tasmania sent a representative military contingent.

2. *Military Cooperation.* In 1894 a first conference was held at the instigation of New South Wales to consider a common structure for all the States' forces and ways of achieving harmonisation and cooperation.

NEW SOUTH WALES

3. *Organisation.* The State's forces consisted of some Permanent (or regular) corps, some partially paid and some volunteer corps (or units). The Permanent ones were one battery of Field Artillery, three companies of Garrison Artillery, some Submarine Miners of the Engineers and a number of Army Service Corps, Ordnance Corps, Medical Staff Corps and Clerks to ensure continuity of effort by the part-time forces. The partially paid element included cavalry and mounted rifles, artillery and engineers, infantry and more support services. The volunteers comprised more infantry, national guards and cadets. The State's contribution to the Jubilee celebrations in England consisted of Lancers, Mounted Rifles, Artillery and Engineers.

4. *Uniform.*

New South Wales Lancers. This Regiment which had earlier had a squadron training in England, sent a detachment of 35 all ranks under Captain C F Cox. Their uniform (see Figs 22 and 33) was a brownish khaki slouch hat with red pagri, the left side turned and secured with the Regimental badge in white metal, and a plume of cock's feathers; leather chinstrap. The tunic was brown with red lancer plastron, red collar, cuffs and piping, and white metal buttons; breeches were brown with a double red stripe; brown leather boots; yellow girdle with two red stripes. Officers' dress was similar with the addition on silver lace. Body lines were white or silver depending on rank.

New South Wales Mounted Rifles. Under their Commanding Officer, Lieutenant Colonel H B Lassetter (see Fig 35), the detachment was of 6 officers and 35 other ranks. The uniform of this Regiment (see Fig 34) was a light khaki slouch hat with khaki pagri, the left side turned up and secured with a white metal badge, and black cock's feathers; leather chinstrap. The light khaki jacket had breast pockets with dark green edging to the turndown collar and the cuffs; dark gren shoulder straps with metal regimental titles. The breeches were light coloured bedford cord. These were worn with brown boots (for other ranks, short boots and long leather gaiters) and equipment.

New South Wales Artillery. The combined representative detachment of Field and Garrison Artillery from New South Wales numbered 2 officers and around 32 other ranks. Their dress was that of the Royal Artillery with local differences, one of which was that the Field branch wore light khaki or stone coloured cord breeches with the blue jacket in Australia (see Figs 51 and 73). However, there is reason to believe that detachments of both branches in London wore the dark blue trousers of the RA with the broad red stripe. The helmet was white with a blue pagri, the upper fold of which was red; the badge on the front was in yellow metal, a cross within a wreath surmounted by a crown; yellow metal curbchain, dome and ball ornament. The tunic was dark blue with scarlet collar and fastened with nine buttons; scarlet piping down the chest and on the rear skirts; the collar was edged all round with yellow cord and the cuffs (blue, unfaced) were edged with the same cord forming an austrian knot above; on the rear skirts two inward facing three-point false pocket flaps were edged scarlet and each had three buttons; buttons and grenade badges on the collar all of yellow metal; blue shoulder straps with yellow edging. Black boots. White buff waistbelt.

New South Wales Engineers. Helmet as for Artillery but with a spike in place of the ball. Royal Engineers pattern tunic: scarlet with dark blue collar and cuffs, fastened down the chest with nine yellow metal buttons; the collar edged all round with yellow cord; the cuffs rising to a shallow point edged with yellow cord forming an austrian knot above; the tunic was edged blue down the chest and all round the skirts, and had two vertical lines of blue piping down the rear skirts from buttons positioned at the waist; shoulder straps in the form of a loop of yellow cord secured with a button. Dark blue trousers with broad yellow stripe. Black boots. White buff waistbelt.

Figure 73. 12 Pdr Gun and Gunners of New South Wales Field Artillery.

QUEENSLAND

5. Organisation. In 1896, the State's forces consisted of a "Defence Force" composed of permanent or regular and militia or partially-paid men, and a Volunteer Force. The total of all was less than 3000 all ranks. The regulars were Headquarters Staff and Artillery; the Militia comprised Mounted Infantry, Artillery, Engineers, Infantry and support services; the Volunteers were composed of infantry and cadets. The State's contribution to the Jubilee celebrations in England was a detachment of Mounted Rifles.

6. Uniform. The Queensland Mounted Rifles (see Figs 39 and 40) wore a khaki slouch hat with a slim plaited pagri; the brim was turned up at the left; plume. Khaki drab jacket with breast pockets brightened with scarlet collar, pointed cuffs and shoulder straps. Matching breeches. Brown leather boots and bandolier. Officers seem to have had gold braid edging to the collar and cuffs, the latter with tracing gold russia braid above and below the point; sam browne belt; pouch belt and pouch.

SOUTH AUSTRALIA

6. Organisation. The State's forces consisted of a small Headquarters Staff and some Artillery, making up the Permanent element; an Active Militia composed of Mounted Rifles (two troops of which at one time seem to have been dressed as Lancers), Artillery, Infantry and support services; there were also Reserve Militia made up of more Mounted Rifles, Infantry and Medical officers. The contribution to the Jubilee celebrations in England was a detachment of 3 officers and 20 other ranks of the Mounted Rifles (see Fig 38 but note that all ranks are wearing the undress pillbox cap).

7. Uniform. Drab helmet with scarlet pagri; yellow metal dome, spike and curbchain, and metal badge in front. Khaki drab jacket with breast pockets, and with scarlet collar and pointed cuffs; metal collar badges (other ranks only). Matching breeches with double red stripes. Brown leather boots and equipment; the waistbelt was of the same proportions as the sam browne and had the same pattern of two pronged buckle; bandolier as for Victoria Mounted Rifles. Officers wore the sam browne belt with its brace.

VICTORIA

8. Organisation. The defence of the Colony was in the hands of Permanent Forces consisting of Headquarters Staff, nearly 300 Artillery personnel, and a small Engineer element; Militia forces consisting of Horse, Field and Garrison Artillery (though the Horse element was disbanded in June 1897), Submarine Mining Engineers, Infantry and support services; and Volunteer forces consisting of Mounted Rifles and Victorian Rangers. The Jubilee contingent was a detachment of the Victoria Mounted Rifles of 4 officers and 48 other ranks.

9. Uniform. Khaki slouch hat with a curious plaited pagri; the right side of the hat was turned up and secured with a cord to a button near the crown; no chinstrap. The jacket had breast pockets and was khaki drab with red collar and pointed cuffs; breeches to match the jacket. Boots and all equipment were brown leather.

WESTERN AUSTRALIA

10. Organisation. Until 1896, the forces of Western Australia were limited to Volunteer Artillery and Infantry. In that year, partially paid Militia were introduced and eventually by 1900, more artillery and infantry had been added and mounted infantry introduced. The Colony's military forces were represented for the Jubilee celebrations in England by two composite detachments drawn form a wide range of small units: Artillery, totalling 2 officers and 10 other ranks, and Infantry, totalling one officer and 22 other ranks.

11. Uniform. See Fig 48.

Perth Artillery Volunteers. It seems that these men brought their own white helmets and belts with them but were issued with new uniform tunics (and perhaps the trousers as well) on arrival in London. Dress: white helmets (probably without pagris) with white metal Royal Artillery Volunteers helmet plate specially made to show "Perth Artillery Vols" on the bottom scroll; white metal curbchain, dome and ball ornament. Uniform as for regular Royal Artillery: blue tunic with scarlet collar, piped scarlet down the chest and on the skirts; yellow cord edging round the collar with yellow metal grenade badges; yellow cord edging the blue (self-material) cuffs and forming an austrian knot above; nine yellow metal buttons down the chest (and 8 more on the skirts behind); blue shoulder straps edged yellow. Black boots. White buff waistbelt with white metal clasp.

Western Australia Infantry Volunteers. For presentational reasons this group was issued with a standard uniform on a similar basis to that of the artillery. Dress: white helmet without pagri; white metal curbchain, dome and spike; white metal helmet plate described as a star surmounted by a guelphic crown with, in the centre, a circlet enclosing a black swan; on the upper part of the circlet the motto "Vigilans" and on the lower five stars. Scarlet tunic with white facings and piping; white metal buttons; dark blue trousers with scarlet welt. Black boots. White buff waistbelt with white metal clasp.

Figure 74. Sergeant Major, Victoria Mounted Rifles.

Appendix 4
Notes on the Canadian Contingent

THE CANADIAN FORCES

1. *Organisational Background*. The military forces of Canada were composed entirely of Militia, of two types, an Active Militia and a Reserve Militia. Within the Active Militia, all corps (or "units", to use the present day term) were formed by voluntary enlistment. A proportion of the Active Militia was permanently embodied in order to provide a training cadre for the remainder (or "Non-Permanent Active Militia" (NPAM)) and to ensure that continuous activity such as supply and repair worked regularly and efficiently. The North West Mounted Police, while semi-military, were a quite separate organisation.

2. *The Canadian Contingent*. The Contingent visiting England (see Fig 30) for the Diamond Jubilee was drawn from the principal arms, as follows:

Commander and other officers	21
Cavalry	51 other ranks
Artillery	28 other ranks
Infantry	77 other ranks
North West Mounted Police	25 all ranks

This produces a total of 192 all ranks. In fact, 202 Canadian personnel were in England and received the Jubilee Medal; the additional 10 are understood to have travelled outside the official arrangements.

CAVALRY

3. *The Regiments*. The permanent force element of the cavalry was called, from 1893, the Royal Canadian Dragoons. The other fourteen Regiments, which are listed below were part-time Militia:

> Governor General's Bodyguard
> 1st Hussars
> 2nd Dragoons
> 3rd Dragoons
> 4th Hussars
> 5th Princess Louise's Dragoon Guards
> 6th Hussars
> 7th Hussars
> 8th Hussars
> 9th Toronto Light Horse
> 10th Queen's Own Canadian Hussars
> 11th Hussars
> 12th Manitoba Dragoons
> King's Canadian Hussars

Of these, the following were represented by small detachments in the Jubilee Contingent: Royal Canadian Dragoons, Governor General's Bodyguard, 1st Hussars, 3rd Dragoons, 5th Dragoon Guards, 8th Hussars, 10th Hussars, 12th Dragoons and King's Canadian Hussars.

4. *Uniforms*. See Fig 32.

Royal Canadian Dragoons (nos 1 and 4): White helmet with yellow metal badge; yellow metal curbchain, dome and spike. Scarlet tunic with dark blue collar and cuffs; the collar edged all round with yellow cord; the shallow pointed cuffs edged with yellow cord which formed an austrian knot above; dark blue shoulder straps edged with yellow cord. Dark blue breeches with broad yellow stripe. Black boots. Sword belt and pouch belt of brown leather. (Note that the cord edgings on the Sergeant Major's tunic (no 1) were gold instead of yellow.)

Governor General's Bodyguard (no 6) (see also Fig 31) White metal helmet with white plume; Dark blue tunic with white collar and blue, self-material, cuffs; tunic edged white down the chest and piped on the rear skirts; the cuffs edged with white cord forming an austrian knot above; the shoulder straps formed of a loop of white cord. Breeches dark blue with a double white stripe. Black boots. White buff sword belt and pouch belt.

1st Hussars (no 9): Busby with white bag and white plume. Jacket as for British Hussars, ie dark blue with yellow cord frogging; white collar. Dark blue breeches with double white stripe. Black boots. White buff sword belt (under the jacket) and pouch belt.

3rd Dragoons (no 5): White helmet with yellow metal badge; yellow metal curbchain, dome and spike. Scarlet tunic with white collar and shallow pointed cuffs; the collar edged all round with yellow cord; the cuffs edged with yellow cord forming an austrian knot above; tunic edged white down the chest and piped on the rear skirts; shoulder straps white edged yellow. Dark blue breeches with double white stripe. Black boots. Brown leather sword belt and pouch belt.

5th Dragoon Guards (no 7): White metal helmet with white plume. Blue tunic with white collar and shallow pointed cuffs; tunic edged yellow down the chest and piped on the rear skirts; cuffs edged with yellow cord forming an austrian knot above; shoulder straps formed of a loop of yellow cord. Dark blue breeches with double white stripe. Black boots. White buff sword belt and pouch belt.

8th Hussars (no 11): White helmet with yellow metal badge, curbchain, dome and spike. Remainder as for 1st Hussars above, except collar edged all round with yellow cord.

10th Hussars (no 10): As for 8th Hussars.

King's Canadian Hussars (no 8): Busby with white bag and plume. Remainder as for 8th Hussars.

Figure 75. Trumpeter, Royal Canadian Artillery.

ARTILLERY

5. *Organisation.* The Artillery Militia consisted of some seventeen field batteries, each of six guns, and some thirty-six companies of Garrison Artillery. Two field batteries were fully manned as permanent force, the remainder of the Artillery being part-time Militia (or NPAM).

6. *Uniform.* As for Royal Artillery (see Bibliography item 16) except that most units wore the white helmet in place of the more normal busby; the Canadians as a general rule did not adopt the blue home service helmet of the British forces. The plate on the white helmet was as for Royal Artillery with the substitution of the word "Canada" for the motto or badge "Ubique"; the same change was made to embroidered embellishments on officers' pouches and sabretaches. Where the busby was worn, for other ranks it was of black fur with a scarlet bag, yellow lines and a white plume in front (see Fig 75); although very like the headdress of the Royal Horse Artillery in Britain, it differed in that it had a yellow cord boss at the front (as for Hussars) and a yellow metal curbchain.

INFANTRY

7. *Organisation.* As in the cavalry, one regiment was permanent force and was entitled the Royal Regiment of Canadian Infantry. The remainder were part-time Militia (or NPAM) and comprised ninety battalions headed by the Governor General's Foot Guards. Unfortunately it is not possible to list so many in this short work. The nominal roll and parent units of all the infantry soldiers who travelled to England has so far eluded research but it seems likely that seventeen regiments sent one or more soldiers.

8. *Uniform.* Uniforms generally, as with the other arms, followed the British practice. In broad essence, there were four styles: the Governor General's Foot Guards; line infantry, sometimes called Grenadiers or Fusiliers; Rifles; and Highlanders. Some examples follow in more detail:

Governor General's Foot Guards. See Fig 26. Other ranks of this Regiment in England wore a fusilier cap with a red hackle on the left, and a yellow metal curbchain; a scarlet tunic similar to that of the Coldstream Guards, that is with buttons in pairs; dark blue trousers with narrow scarlet welt. Officers were dressed as Foot Guards, with a bearskin cap. (Bearskins were issued to other ranks around this time.)

Royal Regiment of Canadian Infantry. See Fig 26. All ranks wore the white helmet with large yellow metal plate or badge, and yellow metal fittings of dome, spike and curbchain. The scarlet tunic was faced dark blue on collar, pointed cuffs and shoulder straps; the collar was piped white along its base, the cuffs were edged with white tubular braid coming to a trefoil above, and the shoulder straps were edged white on the sides; the tunic fastened with seven yellow metal buttons for other ranks (and eight for officers, for whose dress see Fig 78) but note that the soldier wears a protective flap on his left shoulder. Trousers were dark blue with a narrow scarlet welt.

10th Grenadiers. See Fig 26. All ranks wore a bearskin with a red over white hackle, and a yellow metal curbchain (which was probably of infantry pattern or standard 5/8 inch links, rather than the Foot Guards type with graduated links). The tunic was as for the Royal Regiment above, with yellow metal grenade collar badges for other ranks and the unusual feature for non-commissioned officers of wearing their badges on both arms.

62nd Fusiliers. Other ranks wore a fusilier cap with a yellow metal grenade in front and yellow metal curbchain. Tunic and trousers as for the Royal Regiment above.

5th Royal Scots. This Battalion spent the latter part of the 19th Century gradually translating itself into the Black Watch (of Canada). See soldiers in the right background of Fig 30 and the earlier, c 1895, photo at Fig 56. Those travelling to Britain wore the feather bonnet with red hackle, scarlet doublet with blue facings and white braid and piping; black watch kilt; the sporran was very similar to that of the British Gordon Highlanders with a black cantle and white hair with two black tassels; hosetops were diced red and white.

48th Highlanders. Feather bonnet with white hackle; scarlet doublet with dark blue facings and white braid and piping. Kilt of Davidson tartan, that is dark green with broad blue lines forming (approximately 4 inch) squares through each of which run three narrow black lines; a narrow red line through the middle of the broad blue lines. Sporran similar to that of the Cameron Highlanders of the British Army, with black cantle, black hair and two white tassels. Hosetops red and black. Officers wore matching dress (see Fig 77) with gold lace where appropriate; the chief difference was in the sporran which had a white metal cantle and three white tassels on black hair.

2nd Queen's Own Rifles. At home in Canada it seems that this unit wore the old round rifles busby of the 1870s Rifle regiments of Britain with bronzed fittings and a black over scarlet plume. Certainly the Major accompanying the infantry did so — see him sitting on the gun at No 6 in Fig 78 and in front of the group in Fig 26. The rest of his dress was essentially as for the King's Royal Rifle Corps: rifle green tunic frogged with black cord; scarlet facings on collar and cuffs; rifle green trousers with broad black stripe; black patent leather pouch and crossbelt with silver fittings. Other ranks wore the white helmet in Britain with black or bronzed badge and

Figure 76. 48th Highlanders of Canada.

fittings; rifle green tunic and trousers as for King's Royal Rifle Corps; black leather waistbelt with white metal snake clasp and fittings.

3rd Victoria Rifles. As for 2nd Rifles except that all ranks wore the white helmet – see Fig 57. The only significant differences in the dress seem to have been the badges on the headdress and on the pouchbelts worn by officers, warrant officers and sergeants.

POLICE

9. *Organisation.* The North West Mounted Police was raised with a strength of 300 all ranks in 1873. By 1897 it had grown to more than 600 all ranks. It was under the control of the President of the Privy Council of Canada and responsible for keeping order in Manitoba, the North West Territories and the Yukon. The Police was semi-military or what we would now call paramilitary.

10. *Uniform.* The working dress in temperate or warm weather was a drab jacket with brown leather belt and accoutrements. The full dress in which the Jubilee Contingent appeared in London consisted of white helmet, plain scarlet jacket, dark blue breeches with a broad yellow stripe, brown boots and brown leather equipment. (See Fig 30. The 24 representatives of the Police are in the fifth and sixth ranks wearing leather bandoliers over the left shoulder, pistols at their belts and pistol lanyards round the neck.)

Figure 77. Officer, 48th Highlanders of Canada.

Figure 78. Officers of the Canadian Contingent.

Appendix 5
Notes on the Indian Contingents

THE ARMIES OF INDIA

1. *General Background.* In 1897, there were in terms of origin and organisation three armies in India. The Indian Army was a large force composed of regular Indian officers and soldiers commanded and managed by British officers, all funded by the Government of India. There was in addition a Volunteer force of British and Anglo-Indian officers and soldiers. The Indian Government also paid the expenses of keeping a proportion of the British Army in India, totalling in 1897 some 73,000 all ranks. The command structure for this combined force was unified. Thirdly, there existed at the expense of the Indian State rulers their private armies, numbering some 90,000 men in all, of which some 18,000 had been declared for Imperial Service from 1888; that is, they were placed at the disposal of the Government of India.

2. *Organisational Structure of Indian Army.* Because India was such a vast country and because of the way British rule began and developed, Government was for a long time divided between three separate organisations. These were the so-called Presidencies of Bengal, Bombay and Madras. Each had its own Army as well as its civil administration. Late in the 19th Century, Government became centralised though each of the former presidency areas retained its Governor reporting to the Viceroy. From 1895, the Indian Army had been organised on the basis of four Commands, those of the Punjab, Bengal, Bombay (including Aden) and Madras (including Burma). The Regiments of the Indian Army while still retaining titles related to the presidencies could in theory serve anywhere in the sub-continent. They were:

Governor General's (or Viceroy's) Bodyguard
19 regiments of Bengal Cavalry
5 regiments of Punjab Cavalry
Governor's Bodyguard and 3 regiments of Madras Cavalry
Governor's Bodyguard and 6 regiments of Bombay Cavalry
4 regiments of Hyderabad Contingent Cavalry
2 regiments of Central India Horse
45 regiments of Bengal Infantry
10 regiments of Gurkha Infantry
10 regiments of the Punjab Frontier Force
31 regiments of Madras Infantry
26 regiments of Bombay Infantry
6 regiments of Hyderabad Contingent Infantry
Mountain Artillery
Sappers and Miners
Support Services

3. **Diamond Jubilee Contingents.** In response to the invitation of the Home Government it was decided to send two contingents to the Diamond Jubilee celebrations in London. One was to consist of an Indian officer of each of twenty-two Cavalry regiments, usually the senior called the Rissaldar Major. These were to be given the honour of acting as a close escort to The Queen in the Procession. The other contingent was of Indian officers of the Imperial Service troops furnished by Indian States. Led by Maharajah Sir Pertab Singh of Jodhpur, representatives of seventeen States attended and rode in the Procession in a body.

Figure 79. Officers of the Indian Army Contingents with the Band of the Royal Horse Guards in rear, at Windsor 5th July 1897.

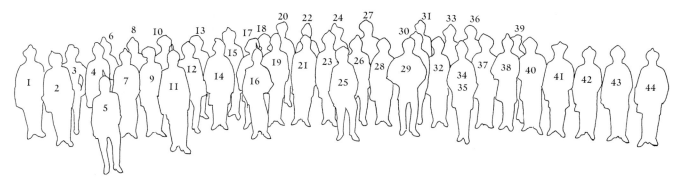

Figure 80. Officers of the Indian Army Contingents at Windsor, 5th July 1897. (See key on page or overleaf, etc)

KEY TO PHOTOGRAPH

1. *Cmdt. Nazir Khan. Rampur I.S Lancers*

2. *Capt Mir Hashim Ali Khan. Hyderabad I.S Lancers*

3. *Cmdt. Rai Bahadur Thakur Dip Singh. Bikanir Ganga Risala*

4. *Risaldar Major Sunayat Singh. Kashmir I.S Lancers*

5. *Major F.H.R. Drummond. 11th [Prince of Wales's Own] Regt of Bengal Lancers*

6. *Cmdt. Chartru Singh. Bhurtpore [now Bharatpur] I.S Lancers*

7. *Cmdt. Abdul Ganny. Gwalior I.S Lancers*

8. *Cmdt. Daud Khan. Ulwar [now Alwar] Lancers*

9. *Cmdt. Govind Ras Matkar. Indore [Holkar's] I.S Lancers*

10. *Risaldar Abdul Majid Khan. Bahawalpur I.S Lancers*

11. *Capt. F Angelo. 9th Regiment of Bengal Lancers*

12. *Cmdt. Mirza Kurim Beg. Bhopal [Victoria] Lancers*

13. *Risaldar Major Didar Singh. Jind I.S Lancers*

14. *Supt. Rai Bahadur Dhunpat Rai. Jeypore [now Jaipur] I.S Transport Corps*

15. *Risaldar Major Kishan Singh. Nabha I.S Lancers*

16. *Unknown British Officer. 11th [POWO] Regt of Bengal Lancers*

17. *Cmdt. Nand Singh. Patiala [Rajindra] I.S Lancers*

18. *Risaldar Dhan Singh. Bhavnagar I.S Lancers*

19. *Risaldar Hara Singh. Kapurthala I.S Lancers*

20. *Jemedar Abdul Karim Khan. The Governor General's [or Viceroy's] Bodyguard*

21. *Risaldar Major Mehrab Ali Khan. 3rd Lancers Hyderabad Contingent*

22. *Risaldar Major Abdul Aziz. 5th Regiment of Bengal Cavalry*

23. *Risaldar Major Sher Singh. 13th [Duke of Connaught's] Regiment of Bengal Lancers*

24. *Risaldar Major Mangul Singh. 3rd Regiment of Bengal Cavalry*

25. *Major A Phayre. 3rd [The Queen's Own] Regt of Bombay Light Cavalry*

26. *Risaldar Major Baha-ud-din Khan. The Central India Horse [ADC to HE the Viceroy]*

27. *Risaldar Major Hukam Singh. 16th Regiment of Bengal Cavalry*

28. *Risaldar Major Izzat Khan. 17th Regiment of Bengal Cavalry*

29. *Capt C.F. Campbell. 6th [The Prince of Wales'] Bengal Cavalry*

30. *Risaldar Kaddam Khan. 4th Regiment of Bengal Cavalry*

31. *Risaldar Major Ali Mohammed Khan. 2nd Regiment of Bengal Cavalry*

32. *Subedar Mohammed Bey. 1st Regiment of Madras Lancers*

33. *Risaldar Mir Haidar Shah. 7th Bombay Lancers [Baluch Horse]*

34. *Lt.Col.J.C.F. Gordon. 6th [The Prince of Wales's] Bengal Cavalry*

35. *Risaldar Makbul Khan. 8th Regiment of Bengal Cavalry*

36. *Risaldar Gurdath Singh. 12th Regiment of Bengal Cavalry*

37. *Risaldar Jehangir Khan. 1st [Duke of Connaught's Own] Bombay Lancers*

38. *Risaldar Net Ram. 7th Regiment of Bengal Cavalry*

39. *Risaldar Major Hussain Khan. 2nd Lancers Hyderabad Contingent*

40. *Risaldar Major Khan Bahadur Khan. 10th Bengal [Duke of Cambridge's Own] Bengal Lancers*

41. *Risaldar Major Faiz Khan. 6th Bombay Cavalry [Jacob's Horse]*

42. *Risaldar Major Mohammed Umar Khan. 5th Bombay Cavalry [Scinde Horse]*

43. *Risaldar Major Kesur Singh. 5th Regiment of Cavalry P.F.F*

44. *Risaldar Nadir Khan. 9th Regiment of Bengal Lancers*

UNIFORMS OF JUBILEE CONTINGENTS

4. *Indian Cavalry.*

Viceroy's Bodyguard. Major Turner, accompanying the Imperial Service Contingent, wore a white helmet with white pagri; gilt curbchain, dome and spike. Scarlet tunic with dark blue collar and cuffs, piped or edged white; down the front eight loops of scarlet cord in line with buttons; on each cuff a scarlet three-pointed slash with simulated buttonholes of scarlet cord and three buttons. Gold shoulder cords and aiguillette. Gold and crimson girdle. Gold lace pouch belt. White breeches. Black boots. A Jemadar wore a dark blue pagri with gold/yellow/dark blue/white stripes; scarlet kurta with gold lace on the collar and surrounding the chest, gold piping on seams, and gold lace and braid on the cuffs. Gold shoulder cords and aiguillette. Gold lace pouch belt with silver fittings. Gold and crimson girdle. Black boots.

2nd Bengal Cavalry. Dark blue pagri with gold/dark blue/grey stripes. Dark blue kurta faced light blue on the collar; gold lace and braid, including tracing around the white metal shoulder chains. Kummerbund scarlet with kashmir end. Waist and pouch belts gold lace with central light of pale blue; silver

Figure 81. Officers of the regular Indian Cavalry. With Lieutenant Colonel Gordon of the 6th Bengal Cavalry at the top and leading they are set out in the same order as they rode in the Procession, see Appendix 1, pages 43/44.

fittings. Black boots.

3rd Bengal Cavalry. Dark blue pagri with gold/light blue/white stripes. Dark blue kurta with yellow facings; gold braid/piping and edging. Scarlet kummerbund with kashmir end. Gold lace waist and pouch belts. Black boots.

4th Bengal Cavalry. Dark blue pagri with gold/dark blue/white stripes (in the photo at Fig 82 the fringe has fallen forward – see Fig 30 for an alternative view). Scarlet kurta faced dark blue; gold lace/braid. Dark blue kummerbund with gold tracery and gold kashmir end. Gold lace on blue leather waist and pouch belts (that is, a blue edging shows). White breeches and black boots.

5th Bengal Cavalry. Dark blue pagri around gold kullah with gold/dark blue/light blue/white stripes. Scarlet kurta faced blue; gold lace/braid. Kummerbund as pagri. Gold lace belts. Black boots.

6th Bengal Cavalry. Lieutenant Colonel Gordon and Captain Campbell were photographed (Fig 81) in a British style of dress: White helmet with pagri coloured gold/yellow in front and blue/white stripes at the sides; gilt curbchain, dome and spike. Dark blue tunic with red facings on collar and cuffs; all embellishments in gold lace or cord (including the unusual cuff decoration called a Bengal knot, a distinction of the Regiments which remained loyal during the Mutiny). Dark blue overalls with double gold stripes. They also had Indian dress (see Fig 80) which was worn for the Procession: Dark blue pagri with gold/dark blue/light blue stripes round a red/gold kullah. Dark blue kurta with red collar and cuffs; gold braid on the collar and cuffs; gold edging to three button front; white metal shoulder chains. Red kummerbund with grey kashmir end. Gold lace belts. White breeches and black boots. For the Procession, Col Gordon's charger had a dark blue shabraque with a double gold braid edging with the Prince of Wales's Plumes over B6C in the rear corners.

7th Bengal Cavalry. Dark blue pagri with gold/blue/white stripes round a red/gold kullah. Scarlet kurta with blue collar; gold braid on collar and front, and gold braid edging to pocket flaps; white metal shoulder chains. Dark blue kummerbund with stripes as the pagri. Gold lace belts. White breeches and black boots.

8th Bengal Cavalry. Dark blue pagri with gold/dark blue/light blue stripes. Dark blue kurta with scarlet collar; gold braid on collar and cuffs; white metal shoulder chains on red backing. Red kummerbund with kashmir end. Gold lace belts. White breeches and black boots.

9th Bengal Lancers. Captain Angelo in British style uniform (see Fig 80) wore a white helmet with white pagri which covered gold cap lines secured underneath and falling behind; gilt curbchain, dome and lancer spike. Dark blue lancer style tunic with white lapels, and white edging and piping; gold lace on collar and cuffs; gold shoulder cords. Pouchbelt of gold lace with central white light. Girdle of gold lace with two crimson stripes. Dark blue breeches with twin gold stripes showing a thin white light between. Black boots. Indian dress worn by Rissaldar Nadir Khan was: dark blue pagri with gold/white stripes. Dark blue kurta with white collar and

cuffs; broad gold braid on the collar, cuffs and down the chest; white metal shoulder chains. Gold lace belts with white central light. Red kummerbund with kashmir end. Tall black boots.

10th Bengal Lancers. Dark blue pagri edged gold with gold/dark blue/white stripes. Dark blue kurta with scarlet collar and cuffs; gold braid on collar, cuffs and front; plain blue shoulder straps. Red kummerbund with kashmir end. Gold lace belts with central crimson light. White breeches and black boots.

11th Bengal Lancers. Major Drummond and another officer of this Regiment wore (see Fig 80) British style dress: white helmet with gold/dark blue/light blue pagri; gilt curbchain, dome and lancer spike. Dark blue lancer stule tunic with scarlet plastron, collar, cuffs, edging and piping; gold lace on collar and cuffs; unusual gold epaulettes with Prince of Wales's feathers in silver at the end; gold girdle with crimson stripes. Gold lace pouch belt with central red light; silver embellishments including Prince of Wales's feathers between boss and pickers. Dark blue breeches with twin gold stripes. Black boots.

12th Bengal Cavalry. Dark blue pagri with gold/dark blue/white stripes. Dark blue kurta faced dark blue with gold braid embellishments; special pattern, narrow, white metal shoulder chains; red kummerbund with kashmir end blocked yellow/green/white/red/blue; gold lace belts. White breeches and tall black boots.

13th Bengal Lancers. Dark blue pagri with gold edges and gold/dark blue/white stripes at the end. Dark blue kurta faced scarlet with silver lace on the collar; white metal shoulder chains; red kummerbund with kashmir end. Silver lace belts with central red light. White breeches and black boots.

16th Bengal Cavalry. Pagri dark blue with gold/dark blue/white stripes. Dark blue kurta with gold lace outlined with tracing braid on the collar, cuffs and down the chest; a single breast pocket on the left was also edged with gold braid; white metal shoulder chains; red kummerbund with gold edging and kashmir ends; gold lace belts. White breeches and black boots.

17th Bengal Cavalry. Dark blue pagri with gold/dark blue/white stripes, round a white kullah. Dark blue kurta with white collar; gold braid on the collar, cuffs and forming elaborate designs on the chest either side of the opening; white metal shoulder chains; blue kummerbund with stripes as the pagri. Gold lace belts. White breeches and black boots.

2nd and 3rd Lancers Hyderabad Contingent. All four Regiments wore uniforms of the same colours at this time, though they varied in the detail of pagri design, the style of lacing on the front of the kurta, and badges. Pagri dark blue with gold/dark blue/white stripes. Dark green kurta faced white with gold lace on the collar and chest; white metal shoulder chains. Cummerbund red with gold edging and kashmir ends. Gold lace belts with a central white light. White breeches and black boots.

5th Punjab Cavalry. Red pagri with gold and black stripes worn over a white pag. Rifle green blouse (that is of the same length as a kurta but opening all the way down); red collar and

Figure 82. (continuation of Figure 81 on page 61)

Figure 83. (conclusion of Figure 81 on page 61)

cuffs; gold lace on collar, cuffs and down the front (as far as the waist), edged with tracing braid; (apparently) gold lace laid on the shoulder straps; red kummerbund with stripes as pagri. Gold lace belts with central red light; the pouch belt had, down the centre, a flask or pistol cord of gold secured at intervals with small, maltese cross, fittings. Curved sabre with mameluke hilt and black scabbard. Scarlet faced sabretache edged with broad gold lace and embroidered with a crown over "PC" reversed over a "V" surrounded with a wreath and battle honours. The pouch was similarly embellished.

1st Madras Lancers. Dark blue pagri with gold/dark blue/light blue/white stripes. French grey (ie light blue) blouse (that is, opening all the way down) with silver lace at the collar; silver lace and tracing braid around the chest; white metal shoulder chains. Dark blue kummerbund with gold tracing and kashmir ends. Dark blue breeches with twin silver stripes. Brown leather belts. Black boots.

1st Bombay Lancers. Dark blue pagri with gold/dark blue/white stripes. Dark green kurta with breast pockets, with scarlet collar and cuffs embellished with gold braid; white metal shoulder chains. Gold cap lines. Red kummerbund with gold edging and kashmir ends. Gold lace belts with central red light. On the pouch belt, silver boss, chain and whistle. White breeches and black boots.

3rd Bombay Cavalry. Major Phayre, soon to be Commandant of the Regiment, wore the British style of uniform for his photograph at Fig 81 but wore Indian uniform for the Procession and the Windsor parade for the Queen (see Fig 80). His British uniform was: white helmet; dark blue pagri with red/blue/white stripes; gilt curbchain, dome and spike. Dark green tunic faced scarlet with gold lace embellishments on collar and cuffs; gold shoulder cords. Dark green overalls with double gold stripes. Gold lace belts with a red light, the pouchbelt embellished with silver boss, chain and whistle. In his Indian dress, he wore: dark blue pagri with coloured stripes; dark green single breasted blouse with scarlet collar and cuffs,

both embellished with gold lace; white metal shoulder chains. Red cummerbund. Belts as above. White breeches and black boots.

5th Bombay Cavalry. Dark blue pagri with gold/dark blue/white stripes. Dark green kurta with white collar; collar and cuffs edged with gold lace; white metal shoulder chains on white backing. Red kummerbund with gold edging and kashmir ends. Gold lace belts with red light. White breeches and black boots.

6th Bombay Cavalry. Dark blue pagri with gold/dark blue/white stripes. Dark green kurta with primrose yellow collar; collar and cuffs edged with gold lace; white metal shoulder chains on yellow backing. Red kummerbund with gold edging and kashmir ends. Gold lace belts with central red light. White breeches with scarlet boots.

7th Bombay Lancers. Light khaki coloured pagri with stripes of gold/dark blue/white. Khaki blouse faced salmon buff on the collar which was edged with gold braid; white metal shoulder chains on yellow backing. Red kummerbund. Brown leather waistbelt. Brown leather pouch belt edged with white metal liked chain with silver embellishments of boss, chain and whistle. Brown leather gauntlets. Khaki breeches and black boots.

Central India Horse. Rissaldar Major Sardar Bahadur Baha-Uddin Khan had joined up in 1851 and was thus in his 46th year of service when he came to England for the Jubilee. His medals recognise service in the Indian Mutiny, China, innumerable Frontier operations and in Afghanistan. He was the holder of the Indian Order of Merit and of the Order of British India with which came the honorific of "Sardar Bahadur". In England he wore not the uniform of the Central India Horse but of an ADC to the Viceroy, described as follows: dark blue pagri with gold/blue/white stripes. Scarlet tunic with dark blue collar and cuffs; red slash piped white on each cuff; eight lines of gold embroidery on the chest, with similar embellishments on the collar, cuffs and skirts: this

Figure 84. Officers of the Indian State Forces. With Rissaldar Thakur Dan Singh of the Babnaghar Lancers at the top and in the lead, they are set out in the same order as they rode in the Procession, see Appendix 1, page 41.

Figure 85. (conclusion of Figure 84 on page 65)

equated to the embroidery on the tunic of an Equerry to the Sovereign but in an Indian motif; gold shoulder cord and aiguillette. Gold and crimson sash over the left shoulder, as for Foot Guards officers. Gold and crimson waist belt and sword slings. Curved sword with mameluke hilt and nickel scabbard. Dark blue overalls with double gold lace stripe, showing a crimson light. Black boots.

5. *Imperial Service Troops*

Jodhpur. In 1897 Colonel Sir Pertab Singh KCSI (see fig 47) was Regent of Jodhpur. He was credited with the formation of the Jodhpur Lancers and latterly with influencing the Rulers to offer the Imperial Service troops to the Government. By 1914, he was an Honorary Major General in the British Army and he accompanied State troops of the Indian Expeditionary Force to France though by then 70 years of age. In 1897 in London he was wearing the uniform of the Jodhpur Lancers: scarlet pagri with white/gold stripes. White kurta with gold lace and embroidery; gold shoulder cords and aiguillette. Scarlet kummerbund with gold figuring and kashmir ends. Gold lace belts with central white light. White breeches with black boots.

Bhavnagar. Dark blue pagri with gold/dark blue/ white/scarlet stripes. Dark blue blouse with red collar and gold lace and braid embellishments; white metal shoulder chains on red backing. Scarlet kummerbund with kashmir ends. Gold lace belts with central red light; silver fittings on pouch belt. White breeches and black boots.

Kapurthala. Blue pagri with gold/dark blue/white stripes. Dark blue blouse with white collar; gold lace and figure braiding on collar, cuffs and chest; white metal shoulder chains. Scarlet kummerbund with gold stripes. Gold lace belts with central white light. Light khaki breeches and black boots.

Jind. Research has not so far yielded a description.

Nabha. Gold pagri with scarlet edging and gold/scarlet/white stripes. Scarlet kurta with gold lace and figure braiding; white metal shoulder chains; blue kummerbund with extensive kashmir design in red, gold and colours. Belts gold lace with central blue light. Breeches appear to be khaki; black boots.

Hyderabad. White pagri with gold/white stripes. Dark green lancer style tunic with white plastron, collar, cuffs, edging and piping; gold lace edging to collar and cuffs; gold shoulder cords; girdle gold and (not known?); gold cap and body lines. White breeches and black boots. Sabretache.

Bahawalpur. Pagri khaki drab with scarlet stripes. Blouse or long tunic of khaki drab with scarlet collar; gold lace, frogging loops and tracing braid on front and sleeves; gold shoulder cords; scarlet kashmir kummerbund. Belts gold with central red light. Khaki breeches and black boots.

Ulwar. Gold pagri with blue stripes. Scarlet kurta with white collar; gold lace and figure braiding to collar, front and cuffs; white metal shoulder chains on white backing; blue kummerbund with gold edging and kashmir ends. Belts gold lace with central blue light. White breeches and black boots.

Bhurtpore. Research has not so far yielded a description. The Bhurtpore Lancers were disbanded in 1899.

Bikanir. Red pagri with gold stripes. Short, tunic length, cream-coloured kurta with scarlet collar; gold lace and figure braiding on collar, cuffs and front; red kummerbund with kashmir ends. Gold lace belts; gilt clasp with white camel badge. White breeches and black boots.

Patiala. (The following is conjectured.) Red and gold pagri. Scarlet kurta with gold lace and figure braiding; white metal shoulder chains; blue kummerbund with gold edging and kashmir ends. Gold lace belts. White breeches and black boots. Sabretache.

Rampur. Dark blue pagri with gold/dark blue stripes. Scarlet kurta with gold lace and figure braiding embellishments; gold shoulder cords; pale blue kummerbund with gold edging and kashmir ends. Red leather belts with two lines of gold lace laid on; silver fittings. White breeches and black boots.

Jaipur. Superintendent Rai Bahadur Dhunpat Rai was an old warrior with service stretching back before the Indian Mutiny of 1857. He alone of the Princely States retainers wears the Order of British India, entitling him to the honorific of Sardar Bahadur. One is tempted to think that he must have possessed medals but possibly had forgotten or lost them! Now he was serving his ruler as Commandant of the Transport Corps and by the end of 1897, it was reported, he was back on the North West Frontier with his men in support of the troops dealing with the Great Frontier War. For his photograph at Fig 85 he seems to be wearing a new but relatively plain kurta. At Windsor on 5th July he was sporting another and altogether more opulent kurta. Details are not known but it is likely that they were both dark green with gold lace and figure braiding embellishments. The pagri was probably green with gold/green/white stripes. Gold lace belts. White breeches with black boots.

Kashmir. Dark blue pagri with gold/blue stripes. Dark blue kurta with scarlet collar; gold lace and figure braiding; red kummerbund with gold/red stripes at the ends. Red leather belts with two lines of gold lace laid on; silver fittings. White breeches and black boots.

Gwalior. Scarlet and gold pagri with gold and blue stripes at the ends. Dark blue lancer style tunic with scarlet collar, plastron, cuffs, edging and piping; gold lace to collar and cuffs; gold shoulder cords. Gold body and caplines. Gold girdle with two crimson lights. Gold lace pouch belt and sord slings with red central light. White breeches and black boots. Sabretache (probably) blue face with gold lace and embroidery.

Indore. Dark blue pagri with gold/dark blue/light blue stripes. Light blue kurta with unusual, apparently self-material, panelling down the chest showing lengths of intricate figure braiding; gold lace on the collar and down the chest; gold lace and figure braiding on the cuffs and around the skirts; red kummerbund. Gold lace belts on red leather. White breeches and black boots.

Bhopal. Dark blue pagri with gold/dark blue/light blue stripes. Dark blue lancer style tunic with buff collar, plastron, cuffs, edging and piping; gold lace to collar and cuffs; girdle possibly gold and another colour (compare with Hyderabad in Fig 84); gold shoulder cords, body and cap lines. Gold lace pouch belt with central white light. White breeches and black boots.

BIBLIOGRAPHY

1. Navy & Army Illustrated – a weekly magazine published from December 1895 by Hudson & Kearns, London

2. Transvaal War Album – a volume of photographs of the British Forces published by Hudson & Kearns, London c 1901

3. Soldiers of the Queen – journal of the Victorian Military Society, quarterly May 1975 to date.

4. Journal of the Society for Army Historical Research, quarterly September 1921 to date. Apply c/o The National Army Museum, London.

5. Military Modelling Magazine – various research articles by R J Marrion and others over the last twenty years.

6. Life at the Court of Queen Victoria, Webb & Bower (Publishers) Ltd, Exeter 1984

7. The Court at Windsor, by Christopher Hibbert, Longmans, London c 1975

8. Illustrated London News – a weekly magazine from 1846

9. Army Lists, various

10. Army Estimates for 1897-98, HMSO, London 1897

11. The Land Forces of the British Colonies and Protectorates, War Office, London 1902

12. Indian Army Uniforms Under The British, by W Y Carman, Volume I by Leonard Hill (Books) Ltd, London 1961 and Volume 2 by Morgan-Grampian, London 1969

13. The Army Book for the British Empire, HMSO, London 1893

14. Uniforms of the Australian Colonies, by A N Festburg and B J Videon, Hill of Content, Melbourne 1971.

15. Military Uniforms from the Collection of the New Brunswick Museum, by David Ross, New Brunswick Museum, Canada 1980

16. Simkin's Soldiers, Volume I The Cavalry and Royal Artillery, by P S Walton, Victorian Military Society 1982

17. Simkin's Soldiers, Volume 2 The Infantry, by P S Walton, Picton Publishing, Chippenham 1986

VICTORIAN MILITARY SOCIETY

The Victorian Military Society is a non-profit organisation based in England whose objects are educational and relate to the study of military affairs during the period 1837 to 1914. In return for an annual subscription, members receive a substantial quarterly illustrated Journal called Soldiers of the Queen and a Newsletter called Soldier's Small Book three times a year. The Society encourages study and communication between its members and to that end sponsors a number of Study Groups focussing on particular camapigns or subjects. For more information, please contact the Publicity Officer VMS, 20 Priory Road, Newbury, Berkshire RGI4 7QN, England.

Figure 86 (above left). Field Marshal HRH The Prince of Wales KG, the principal organiser of the Diamond Jubilee Celebrations. King of Great Britain and Ireland and Emperor of India from 22nd January 1901.

Figure 87 (above right). Her Majesty Queen Victoria 1897